SPIRITUAL LEADERSHIP,

RESPONSIBLE MANAGEMENT

MICHAEL T. DIBBERT

SPIRITUAL LEADERSHIP,

RESPONSIBLE MANAGEMENT

*A Guide for Leaders
of the Church*

**Ministry
Resources
Library**

Zondervan Publishing House • Grand Rapids, MI

SPIRITUAL LEADERSHIP, RESPONSIBLE MANAGEMENT
Copyright © 1989 by Michael T. Dibbert

MINISTRY RESOURCES LIBRARY is an imprint of Zondervan Publishing House,
1415 Lake Drive S.E., Grand Rapids, Michigan 49506.

Library of Congress Cataloging in Publication Data

Dibbert, Michael T.
   Spiritual leadership, responsible management.

   1. Church management. I. Title.
BV652.D46   1988   254   88-26691
ISBN 0-310-52031-2

Edited by Joan Johnson and Michael G. Smith
Designed by Louise Bauer

Printed in the United States of America

91 92 93 / EP / 8 7 6 5 4 3 2

To Tricia,
my faithful wife

Contents

PART IV

Introduction

This book is not an attack on modern management theory, large churches, or pastors who read books like *In Search of Excellence, The Effective Executive,* and *The One Minute Manager*. Already, too many people question the validity of using business techniques and tools in church work. Some have gone as far as to say that the church's current interest in management is one of the primary reasons for the "dearth of spiritual leadership and direction in the evangelical world" today.[1] Ironically, many of these same people often complain that the church is disorganized and that very little is accomplished.

Neither is this book a defense of "the New Testament church" concept and the notion that "small is beautiful." Managing a large church is obviously a greater challenge than managing a small church, but it doesn't have to be a nightmare. Large churches can retain a sense of community and enjoy rich fellowship—if they work at it. But small churches have to work toward deep unity too. As many pastors will testify, managing even a small church can be a headache! So "big" is not necessarily better, but neither is it inherently bad.

Furthermore, even though the New Testament offers principles of church life (e.g., its mission, the qualifications and responsibilities of leaders, spiritual gifts), God has not called the church in the twentieth century to duplicate the experience of first-century saints. The culture and times in which we live are very different.

Consider, for example, the element of size. The average church in American today has a congregation of approximately two hundred members.[2] By contrast, most believers in the early church met in "house churches," which, according to biblical scholars, could accommodate around forty people (Acts 2:42; Romans 16:10–11).[3] There were, of course, larger churches in cities like Jerusalem, Rome, and Corinth, but most were small by today's standards. Does that mean that we should abandon our facilities and meet only in homes? Of course not!

The simple truth is that churches today, like churches in the first century, are organizations. Like other organizations, they need to be managed (that is, guided, directed, and led). The question is not if, but how it should be done. How a church is managed is pivotal to the life of the body. Leaders need to remember that a proper "attitude about ministry and approach to ministry is more important than a lot of canned expertise," according to Richard Halverson.[4]

After all, churches are not business corporations, and they should not be managed as such. Those that are managed as a corporation tend to die a slow death spiritually, if not numerically. This does not mean, however, that pastoral leaders can afford not to study business principles of management. W. Ward Gasque, professor of New Testament at Regent College, has aptly noted that "one of the most striking features of *In Search of Excellence* is the way it is filled with scriptural teaching without being even slightly aware of the fact."[5]

Although they share some characteristics, pastoral leaders and business managers have significantly different functions and significantly different methods to carry them out. Yet the Bible does not present one particular model of managing the church to which all must adhere. Rather, the Bible shows how God's people (for example, Moses, Nehemiah, David, Paul, and Peter) have effectively dealt with multiple management responsibilities in varying circumstances.

In addition to examining many of these biblical situations, the solutions offered, and the management principles behind them, I have included insights from current management theory and practice. The goal of this coupling is to assist pastoral leaders in effectively managing their ministries while applying biblical precepts.

As an elder in the local church I have grappled with many of the issues presented in these pages. I have firsthand experience, for instance, with the problems of planning, the difficulty of delegating, and the challenge of coordinating ministries of a growing church.

As one who earns his living in business I understand how tempting it is to superimpose commercial management methods on church life out of a genuine desire to complete a task. I also know how humbling it is to be thought of as heavy-handed and task-oriented rather than democratic and people-oriented.

Earnestly seeking help, I have dealt with the disappointment of reading "Christian" management books, only to find that they are based on business management models and emphasize practices that do not correspond with the nature and purpose of the local church.

As a seminary graduate who later earned an MBA degree (Master of Business Administration), I am also thoroughly convinced that few church leaders are adequately prepared to deal with the management responsibilities they invariably encounter.

Fortunately, the Bible isn't silent on the subject of how to manage the ministry. The word "manage" is seldom used in Scripture, but words like "body," "shepherd," "steward," "elder," "administer," and "lead" abound with management implications.

The purpose of this book, then, is to provide practical help. I want to show pastoral leaders—clergy and laity alike—how they can effectively deal with their ministry-related management responsibilities. This can be done without becoming mired in management theory or administrative details and without the church's losing its sense of community.

To do this in a meaningful and interesting way, I have developed a case study, which is introduced in chapter 1. It is a composite of real-life situations drawn from my own pastoral ministry and the experiences of several other shepherds who are ministering in a variety of churches with different denominational affiliations. The names of individuals involved and the details of certain events have been changed to guarantee anonymity. The case study, while not exhaustive, touches on many genuine management issues that church leaders face. As the book unfolds, the case study will be enlarged and the distinctive qualities of management in the church will become clear.

NOTES

1. Walter A. Elwell, ed., *Evangelical Dictionary of Theology* (Grand Rapids: Baker, 1985), 2:1046–50.
2. Constant H. Jacquet, Jr., *Yearbook of Canadian and American Churches 1985* (Nashville: Abingdon, 1985), 236–37.
3. F. F. Bruce, *New Testament History* (New York: Anchor, 1972), 394.
4. Richard Halverson, "Planting Seeds and Watching Them Grow," *Leadership* (Fall 1980): 12–23.
5. W. Ward Gasque, "The Church in Search of Excellence, Why the Infatuation With Management Books?" *Christianity Today* (15 February 1985): 54–56.

PART I

Chapter 1

Case Study:
Trinity Evangelical Church

When Tom resigned to go to mission candidate school in Chicago, the board of elders* at Trinity Evangelical Church (hereafter referred to as "Trinity") wasn't completely surprised. Tom had been an associate pastor at Trinity for several years, and they knew he'd leave shortly after he finished seminary.

No one, however, thought he would leave so quickly. His sudden departure left the elders unprepared for the issues that surfaced while they discussed how to replace him.

In addition to being an elder, Tom had been responsible

---

*Elder rule is frequently found in evangelical churches, but readers should note that information presented in subsequent chapters will be applicable regardless of a church's form of government.

for the church's small-group ministry and Christian education program. He also counseled frequently. He and his wife Mary were well-liked by many in the church. The couple would be sorely missed as well as difficult to replace!

From the start, one of the primary candidates for Tom's job was Richard, currently the church's part-time minister to collegians. Richard wanted a full-time position with the church and was willing to assume responsibility for small groups. Although the college ministry had blossomed under his direction, Richard did not know much about small groups, and even if the church hired him full-time they would have to find someone else to oversee Christian education. Furthermore, several of the elders were not sure that the church could justify (or afford) having a full-time staff person just for small groups and the college ministry when other areas in the church were understaffed and underfunded.

For example, John, the senior pastor, had been spending much time on church finances and administration. Although he never complained, everyone knew it was wearing on him; it showed in the quality of his sermons and his countenance. John was an effective pastor and a well-organized person, but financial management and church administration were not his strengths. As a result of John's extensive involvement with the church's finances, some of the elders had come to the conclusion that the church needed a full-time bookkeeper and/or administrator.

Other members of the congregation believed the church needed a full-time youth pastor so that it could start attracting more families with children. Many legitimate needs called for attention. It was hard to know which ones deserved priority.

Along with forcing the elders to examine staff roles and evaluate the needs of various ministries, Tom's departure also prompted them to ponder why the board had such a difficult time gaining new elders. Although they solicited recommendations from church members and tried to identify everyone with "leadership potential," they seldom identified more than two or three viable candidates, who were invariably either too busy to serve or didn't think they were qualified.

The board had managed to survive with five elders for some time, two of whom were on staff. But with Tom leaving there would be only four, and one of the nonstaff elders was moving soon. It just seemed as if a church with more than five hundred members should have more people willing and able to serve as elders.

The more the board talked about the difficulty of finding new elders, the more they realized that many projects and goals had never been realized. The church newspaper had never been established well; there was little outreach into the community; the visitors' ministry was struggling. There just weren't enough people willing to help.

And it wasn't as though the elders hadn't tried to "unleash the church" and "liberate the laity."[1] Shortly before Tom announced his resignation, the elders established several ministry groups and appointed deacons to help in matters like maintenance, evangelism, and missions. Unfortunately, few people followed through, and the ministry groups never developed. That was discouraging to everyone.

The church seemed to be at a crisis point. Tom was leaving soon, and people were complaining about the elders not communicating with the congregation. The elders needed to make some decisions—quickly. Finding that they didn't have time to discuss such issues at their weekly board meetings, one of the elders suggested that they hold an extended planning meeting on a Saturday morning.

No one could remember the last time there had been such a planning meeting. To one elder, however, it was reminiscent of a time when the church was smaller and everyone was involved—the "good old days."

Somewhere along the way, the elders lost sight of why they became elders in the first place. Maybe the building program had taken more out of them then they realized. Who knows? Whatever it was, many of the elders felt they had lost their initial vision for the church. They had lost the sense of expectancy they used to have. As one elder put it, "the ministry isn't as fulfilling as it used to be."

NOTES

1. These expressions are borrowed from Frank Tillapaugh, *The Church Unleashed* (Ventura, Calif.: Regal, 1982), and J. Paul Stevens, *Liberating the Laity* (Downers Grove, Ill.: InterVarsity, 1985). These are insightful books on the role of the laity in the ministry.

Chapter 2

The Church's Management Dilemma

The church's survival is a sign of God's existence. No other enterprise run so poorly could stay in business.

Henry Ford

Most feel qualified to provide spiritual leadership, but not many are adequately prepared to manage an organization.

Myron Rush
Management: A Biblical Approach

The case study of Trinity Evangelical Church offers a glimpse of a spectrum of management issues pastoral leaders frequently encounter. It includes facets like selecting staff, training people to minister, planning, working with people, coordinating programs, and managing the church's mission.

Although situations like the one that developed at Trinity occur frequently, they do not usually reach a crisis point—

19

when something *must* be done—unless the church experiences a major change.

For Trinity, the resignation of a key staff person was the catalyst for the explosion. Other factors being equal, had Tom stayed, the church might have continued in the same operating procedures indefinitely. In other churches the retirement of a dearly loved senior pastor, the undertaking or completion of a building program, a major growth spurt, or a significant congregational controversy can expose the need for change.

In the absence of such watershed events (and the organizational change and uncertainty that accompany them), a surprising number of churches muddle along. And the church, which by nature is a resilient organism, may continue to grow. Members may even be satisfied. But the tragedy is that, despite the symptoms of well-being, the church has achieved only a fraction of its potential.

WHY MANAGEMENT CRISES ARE COMMON

Churches do not struggle with management-related issues simply because pastoral leaders are disorganized or overworked (which is not to say that there are not some disorganized and overworked pastoral leaders out there). Nor is it because pastoral leaders don't recognize some of the problems or want to solve them. John, Trinity's senior pastor, sensed that something was amiss and was doing his best to improve the situation by taking care of the church's finances. It was an area he was not qualified to deal with, and he did not enjoy it; but as he often said, "Someone's got to do it."

There are many reasons why churches struggle with management-related issues. One of the biggest problems is that few pastoral leaders are trained to deal with the management responsibilities they encounter. I know, you think I'm joking. But do you know how many courses related to church administration or management your pastor took when he was in seminary? Probably none. The seminary I attended required only one two-hour course on church administration, and half of it was devoted to Christian education.

It doesn't appear that much has changed since I graduated from seminary. In my research for this book I checked the course catalogs of a number of seminaries. Very few offered courses in church management. If this limited survey reflects what most seminaries offer, there is a serious lack of preparation for management.

The problem, of course, isn't just that seminaries do not provide adequate training. Even if more courses were offered, many students would bypass them unless they were mandatory. After all, the reason these students attend seminary in the first place is to learn how to preach, teach, and be "fishers of men" (Matthew 4:19). This is a good reason for going to seminary, but it is not good enough. Eugene Peterson, pastor of Christ Our King Church in Bel Air, Maryland, states, "Pastoring in the twentieth century requires two things: one, to be a pastor, and two, to run a church."[1] An effective pastor needs to know something about management.

"But," you protest, "our church has several business people on the board who can take care of the church's management needs."

This is a common assumption. But it's false. Think for a moment. How many of these business people have practical ministry experience and understand (1) the purposes of the church, and (2) their personal role in the church in light of that purpose? Lyle Schaller has shown us a painful truth: good intentions and personal godliness notwithstanding, most laypersons take passive roles, rubber-stamping staff recommendations.[2] Worse than a passive laity, according to many pastors, is a laity mindlessly resistant to any innovation for the sake of preserving "tradition."

Furthermore, successful business people aren't always good managers. In fact, many are utterly lost in the task of managing a spiritual community. Why? The nature and level of their skills in such matters as accounting, law, or real estate are often quite sophisticated and of little practical value to the ongoing operations of the church. For instance, one of the elders at Trinity, a highly respected tax attorney and a very capable fund-raiser, openly admitted he knew very little about the church and almost nothing about management.

"So," you ask, "how did he become an elder?" Good question. The answer to that is the subject of chapter 14. For now, I'll rest my case and reiterate my point. The major reason churches struggle with management-related issues is that few pastoral leaders are trained to deal with them. It is not the only reason, but it is the most significant.

PROBLEMS GENERATED BY IGNORING BIBLICAL PRINCIPLES OF MANAGEMENT

Any church that continually ignores biblical principles of management will sooner or later encounter problems similar to the ones at Trinity. Consider the problem of elder burnout. The elders simply had too much to do—a common situation.

Moses had a similar problem some 3,500 years ago (Exodus 18:13–26). He was the sole judge for an entire nation! People had to wait a long time to see him. It is no wonder they all were exhausted! The solution was simple. Jethro, his father-in-law, suggested that Moses delegate some of his work to others. Simple? You bet. The beauty of the plan was not just its simplicity—it also worked! Now consider the case study. Perhaps if the Trinity elders had encouraged Tom to delegate some of his work, he would have stayed longer.

Trinity's problem, of course, was a little more complicated than Moses' situation. At least Moses was able to find people to help him. Many of those nominated to serve as elders at Trinity did not think they were qualified. Do you know what was holding them back? Most of them thought they lacked the Bible knowledge and ministry experience necessary to do a good job. This underscored the fact that the pastoral leaders at Trinity were failing to train people for ministry (Ephesians 4:11–16). The ministry groups' failure to thrive was additional evidence of this. Yet even then, the elders were surprised to see this occur. It is obvious they just couldn't see the problem. This myopia is all too common.

Neglecting to train others for ministry was a significant error of the elders. But an even more crucial omission in their management of a spiritual community was their ignoring the church's mission. When Trinity was founded, the elders clearly believed that God had called them to a unique ministry. They felt that the land their church was built on was a miraculous gift from God, and they were totally committed to exalting his name by (1) edifying the saints, and (2) evangelizing non-Christians.

Unfortunately, as the church grew and some founding board members moved away, the elders became preoccupied with the details of budgeting and building programs. Now, handling finances in a godly way and providing the saints a place to meet are important matters, but they're not nearly so important as responding to God's purpose for his children. This was the pivotal mistake at Trinity.

PROBLEMS GENERATED BY ADOPTING NONBIBLICAL MANAGEMENT METHODS

In subsequent chapters we will look closely at some important biblical principles of management. Before doing so, however, a word of caution is appropriate: worse than ignoring biblical principles of management is indiscriminately applying management methods drawn from military or business models. Most church members are not expecting their pastoral leaders to emulate the leadership-management styles of General George Patton or automobile executive Lee Iacocca. What they want are good shepherds (1 Peter 5:1–5). Yet a surprising number of pastoral leaders, frustrated with an inefficient organization, succumb to acting like autocratic army officers and business executives.

Consider a few examples. At one point Trinity was running short on small group leaders. People were forced to wait up to six months to join a group. This was so discouraging that the elders decided to do two things. First, they pressured three groups to split and add new members. Second, they told group leaders that all groups must have at least thirty members (which would completely change the dynamics of the groups). Group leaders weren't consulted or drawn into the decision-making process; they were simply informed by letter of the board's decision.

The results were not edifying. Several groups resisted. A few people left the church. And the elders were criticized for being dictatorial. So much for "strong leadership."

Undaunted by the resistance they met in "solving" the small-group problem, the elders forged ahead to tackle the leadership drought. But instead of taking time to groom mature men and women for significant ministry responsibilities, they hurriedly singled out "sharp" people and gave them impressive titles and positions in the church, thereby ignoring Paul's admonition not to lay hands on a person too quickly (1 Timothy 5:22). Of course, when the sharp people failed to perform as hoped, the elders were completely surprised.

Trinity's problems are not unique. Many senior pastors eventually conclude that if they want anything done, they will have to do it themselves. Then they proceed without consulting anyone. Later, after they've been asked to resign, they are shocked to find out that many people thought they were domineering, hard to talk to, and manipulative.

A pastor's forced resignation is not the only negative outcome of this type of management style. When a church overloads the senior pastor with management responsibilities, everyone loses. Paul Anderson, pastor of Trinity Lutheran Church in San Pedro, California, has pointed out, "A church run in an authoritarian way will receive only the part of the Spirit's guidance that one man is able to receive."[3]

Poor management also affects the way groups within the church operate. For example, instead of waiting on the Lord to work in the hearts of its members, a board may adopt a majority-vote policy for decision making and move ahead with a project even when there is a serious lack of unity on it. Later, when they encounter difficulties and the congregation's enthusiasm wanes, they wonder why.

Stymied in their attempts to help church members develop ministry skills, and discouraged by the time and effort needed to coordinate "volunteers," numerous churches resort to using "contract labor"—that is, they create many little part-time positions. This further undermines the willingness of laypeople to assume significant church responsibilities. The result is that many church members don't use their spiritual gifts, and neither they nor the church realize their growth potential.

As we have seen, the cure (adopting nonbiblical management methods) is often as bad as the disease (ignoring biblical principles of management). The solution to the church's management dilemma, however, is not to ignore it in hope that somehow it will all work out. No, ignoring management responsibilities only creates bigger problems.

No single step can solve the church's management dilemma, but the starting point is for pastoral leaders (staff and lay leaders alike) to understand clearly the purpose of the church and the role that all pastoral leaders (not just the staff) have in managing the ministries of the church.

For many pastoral leaders this will require taking a fresh look at Scripture and stepping back to rethink how their church operates. For others, it will mean giving up some autonomy, control, and power. In many cases, it will require the laity to take more active leadership roles in the church.

Coming to grips with the issues presented in this book may be difficult, but in the long run it will lead to a higher quality of life in the body of Christ and a greater amount of light in the world (Matthew 5:16).

NOTES

1. "Haphazardly Intent: An Approach to Pastoring," an interview with Eugene Peterson in *Leadership* (Winter 1981): 12–24.

2. Lyle Schaller, *Activating the Passive Church* (Nashville: Abingdon, 1982).

3. Paul Anderson, "Who's in Charge Here," *Pastoral Renewal* (June 1985): 161, 172–74.

Chapter 3

Managing a Spiritual Community

If anyone does not know how to manage his own family, how can he take care of God's church? (1 Timothy 3:5)

Christ is the head of the church, his body, of which he is the Savior. (Ephesians 5:23)

Long after I became actively involved in the local church, I enrolled in an intensive MBA program at Southern Methodist University. I knew the courses would be difficult, and I was quite apprehensive, especially since I had no background in business.

So I brushed up on my math, read some business periodicals, prayed more fervently than I had in some time, and with great fear and trembling jumped right in. In no time at all I was in way over my head, but by the grace of God I survived and went on to graduate. Looking back, what

METROPOLITAN COLLEGE
ELIZABETH BRASWELL PEARSALL LIBRARY

shocked me the most about business school was not the intricacies of accounting or finance. Nor was it the "secularism" on campus. What troubled my mind and affected my emotions the most was an introductory management course, affectionately called "Organizational Behavior and Administration 521."

The course's subject matter wasn't disturbing in and of itself. What bothered me was seeing the pervasive use of the business management techniques within the church. I saw the tragedy of churches like Trinity deciding, albeit innocently, to operate like corporations. And I saw them doing so without ever realizing all that would be sacrificed by making that decision.

COMMUNITY ... OR CORPORATION?

Consider how corporations determine the success of their operations. Although other factors are regarded, in the final analysis the success of a business enterprise is measured by "the bottom line," tangible profits benefiting management and shareholders.[1]

Unfortunately, when issues became complicated at Trinity, the elders also started focusing on quantitative measures of success (such as donations and attendance). Steady growth in attendance and donations was considered solid "evidence" that the church was healthy. The fact that little was being done to equip the saints and evangelize non-Christians didn't seem to matter.

Fortunately, an increasing number of church-renewal leaders have shown that the fruitfulness of a church and its ministries cannot be measured by numbers alone.[2] Much of what pastoral leaders have been called to do involves long-term attitudinal and behavioral changes that defy precise measurement or quantification. After all, how does one measure the faith, hope, and love in a church community? (See 1 Corinthians 13:13.) You simply know it when you experience it. The irony of events at Trinity is that while attendance at worship services increased, the degree to which church members were using their spiritual gifts in mutual ministry actually decreased.

John's role at Trinity was also more characteristic of a business executive than a pastoral leader. Although the church extolled the virtues of elder rule and the priesthood of all believers, in reality "the buck stopped" with John. He set the agenda and led the elder meetings. He had final say in who was hired or fired. His opinions determined whether or not new ministries would be supported.

In short, as a result of other elders' defaulting on their responsibilities, John essentially became the chief executive officer of Trinity Evangelical Church. And the Lord Jesus Christ, who has never abrogated his position as head of the church, began receiving less than the full glory and honor he deserves (Ephesians 5:23). Consolidating authority to one person or a select few skews the line of responsibility within the church, thereby dimming the glory of Christ in this world. Each member of the body needs to depend fully on Jesus to accomplish particular tasks. If only a few have a task to accomplish, only a few experience this dependence on Christ. If only a few depend on Jesus, then the full power of Christ is not seen. We all need to see Christ as the force that moves within us to move the entire body.

The best way to avoid what happened at Trinity is for pastoral leaders to remember that their church really is "the body of Christ" (Ephesians 4:12). Jesus—not the senior pastor—is the head of the church, and church members need to be encouraged to keep their focus on him.

Church members also need to remember that they are members of one another, and that the Holy Spirit has given gifts to each member for the building up of the body (Romans 12:5; 1 Corinthians 12:12–31). A major reason why the church is often referred to as a "community" in this book is that the Holy Spirit united each Christian with God and other believers in the body of Christ, thereby creating a spiritual community of saints, a living organism. It is a distinctiveness that transcends denominational differences and establishes

28

the basis of our relationships as brothers and sisters who share life together in the Lord (Ephesians 5).

Figure 3-1 highlights some of the basic differences between a church community and a business corporation.

Figure 3-1
Church Community–Business Corporation

Element	Church Community	Business Corporation
1. Major leader	Jesus Christ	CEO/president
2. Mission	Worship Edification Evangelism	Profit Create jobs Provide goods/services
3. Measure of success	Attitudinal and behavioral change Qualitative Subjective	"Bottom line" Quantitative Objective
4. Basic nature	Organism (body)	Institution
5. Membership	Voluntary Very diverse (Cradle to grave)	Economic necessity Mostly adults
6. Relationships among members	Equals Familial "Brothers and sisters"	Definite hierarchy Based on power, control, authority
7. Organizational structure	Elder rule Congregational Bishopric	Functional Market Matrix
8. Policies and procedures	Biblical	Established by the corporation

PASTORAL LEADER* ... OR MANAGER?

Given the basic differences between a church community and a business corporation, one would expect the

---

*The term "pastoral leaders" refers to both paid and nonpaid church leaders. It is broader in scope than the term "elder" or "deacon," and it applies to anyone significantly involved in the ministry of the local church.

qualifications and operating style of their respective leaders to differ (fig. 3-2). They do. Consider the issue of qualifications.

In the business world most people qualify for a certain position on the basis of their education, experience, or training. In the local church the key issues are (1) character, and (2) giftedness. The primacy of character is covered in passages like 1 Timothy 3:1–13 and Titus 1:5–9. The importance of God-given spiritual gifts is described in Ephesians 4:1–16. (See also 1 Corinthians 12.) A person's spiritual gifts, such as the gifts of pastor-teacher, determine one's ministry in the church rather than one's education!

One of the reasons the board at Trinity ran into serious problems is that several of the elders had been selected on the basis of their social status and business qualifications (for example, education and experience). To be sure, they were older and they were successful (economically), but they did not know what their spiritual gifts were, and they were seldom involved in practical ministry.[3]

The manner in which pastoral leaders and business managers endeavor to fulfill their responsibilities is also very different. Christ was adamant about pastoral leaders not acting like worldly authorities (Luke 22:24–30). Instead of "lording" power over others (for example, dominating or controlling), pastoral leaders are to be servants and shepherds of God's flock (Mark 10:45; 1 Peter 5:1–4).[4] It is a style of leadership that requires helping others grow, being sensitive to the needs of individuals, and recognizing that the Holy Spirit is the agent of change. Furthermore, an effective pastoral leader must understand the importance of modeling and must know the people to whom one is ministering (1 Corinthians 11:1).

Business managers seldom have an opportunity to develop such relationships with their employees, and in many cases corporate policy explicitly prohibits their doing so. This does not mean that business managers are totally insensitive and uncaring. Most of the business managers I know who are working in large corporations sincerely value good relationships and fair treatment. But they have a certain job to do, and in the final analysis the task takes precedence over the person.

Figure 3-2
Pastoral Leaders–Business Managers

Element	Pastoral Leader	Business Manager
1. Primary qualifications	Character, giftedness	Training, skills
2. Basic responsibility	Equip Nurture Teach Counsel Model	Perform Plan, control, lead, evaluate
3. Descriptive "titles"	Steward Shepherd Servant	Manager, director, supervisor
4. Style of operating	Relational grace	Results-oriented works
5. Accountability	To God and to other members of the body	To superiors, governing board
6. Incentives	Spiritual blessings Altruism	Income, status, job satisfaction

MANAGEMENT FUNCTIONS OF PASTORAL LEADERS

Most pastoral leaders are uncomfortable using the term "management" in relation to their pastoral ministries. After all, the word "management" never occurs in the Bible. (The term "Trinity" never appears in the Bible either!) Does the word have any legitimacy in the church? Let's decide that by looking at its derivation.

The English word "manage" derives from the French word *manège,* which originally meant "to train (a horse) in his paces," "to cause to do the exercises of *le manège,*" or riding school. Hence, the words "manage" and "management" are usually defined by using the terms "lead," "guide," or "direct."[5]

Two biblical terms closely correspond to the English word "manage." The first is *oikonomia*, usually translated "stewardship."[6] In New Testament times a "steward" was essentially a business manager; he was responsible for faithfully managing his master's business affairs. "Stewardship" was a familiar concept in the ancient world and became an important image in the teachings of Jesus, Paul, and Peter (Luke 12:41–48; 1 Corinthians 4:1–2; 9:16; Colossians 1:24–26; 1 Peter 4:10).

The second biblical word is *prohistēmi*.[7] It is actually translated "manage" in 1 Timothy 3:4–5 (NIV and NASB). In that context Paul implies that if a man does not know how to manage his own family he won't know how to manage the church. (See also 1 Timothy 5:17.)

In Romans 12:8 the same word is translated "leadership" (NIV) and "lead" (NASB). The basic idea being asserted is that one should lead (that is, be concerned about, care for, give aid) with diligence.[8] Thus, biblically speaking, the word "manage" means "lead, guide, direct, and care for." Obviously there is a place for this concept in God's church.

In the following chapters several of the key—and problematic—management functions of pastoral leaders will be discussed. Understanding the nature and needs of your community are essential to the accomplishment of your church's unique calling.

NOTES

1. Cecily C. Selby, "Better Performance From Non-Profits," *Harvard Business Review* (September–October 1978): 92–98. An interesting article that highlights some of the basic differences between "non-profit" and "for-profit" institutions.

2. Gene Getz's *Sharpening the Focus of the Church* (Chicago: Moody, 1985) and Larry Richards's *A Theology of Church Leadership* (Grand Rapids: Zondervan, 1980) should be required reading for pastoral leaders. I don't agree with everything they say, but their insights into Scripture and the local church are invaluable.

3. A number of people who serve on church boards are also directors or trustees of other nonprofit organizations. The typical nonprofit organization has an average of thirty board members, most of whom are responsible for fund-raising. Unfortunately, many believers adopt similar roles on church boards. For a fuller discussion, see Israel Unterman and Richard Davis, "The Strategy Gap in Not-for-Profits," *Harvard Business Review* (May–June 1982): 30–40.

4. D. Edmond Hiebert, "Counsel for Christ's Undershepherds: An Exposition of 1 Peter 5:1–4," *Bibliotheca Sacra* (October–December 1982): 330–41. This is a thorough discussion of the responsibilities of pastoral leaders.

5. *Webster's New World Dictionary*, College Edition (New York: World, 1968), 889.

6. Walter Bauer, *A Greek-English Lexicon of the New Testament and Other Early Christian Literature*, trans. W. F. Arndt and F. W. Gingrich (Chicago: University of Chicago Press, 1957), 562.

7. Ibid., 713–14.

8. Stephen B. Clark, *Patterns of Christian Community* (Ann Arbor, Mich.: Servant, 1984), 15–26.

PART II

Chapter 4

Mission: The Purpose of the Local Church

Every church, large or small, rural or urban, will function more effectively by clearly defining its mission.

Alvin J. Lindgren
Management for Your Church

"Therefore go and make disciples of all nations, baptizing them in the name of the Father and of the Son and of the Holy Spirit, and teaching them to obey everything I have commanded you. And surely I am with you always, to the very end of the age."

(Matthew 28:19–20)

Most Christian organizations result from God's giving a person or a small group of people a sense of calling or purpose about something that needs to be done. Exact blueprints are seldom if ever provided, but the Spirit does guide and direct the saints as they respond to God's working in their lives.

The founders of Trinity Evangelical Church clearly sensed that God had called them to a special ministry. Their property, located near a large university, put them in a prime position to minister to thousands of college students. Many of these were international students who would one day become leaders in their own countries.

In addition to a plentiful "harvest," Trinity was fortunate to have several church members who had extensive practical ministry experience with college ministries such as the Inter-Varsity Christian Fellowship. They were dedicated to exalting God through the church by (1) edifying the saints, and (2) evangelizing non-Christians.

It was an exciting combination: fields ready for harvesting, workers with a clear sense of direction and purpose, and an expectant body trusting in God. And God's blessing was on it all. Many people came to know the Lord, members of the church ministered to one another, and the church grew rapidly. No church could have asked for a better start.

Why was it, then, that within four to five years, the elders at Trinity found themselves saddled with details and discouragement, without any clear sense of direction or purpose?

ORIGINS OF CONFUSION AND DISCOURAGEMENT

First of all, as a result of Trinity's rapid expansion (an event no one could have foreseen) the elders used most of their time trying to decide how to cope with the church's growth (for example, where to meet, how to organize the Sunday school, how to hire additional staff). The issues were important and not easy to delegate. Unfortunately, the more time the elders spent dealing with logistical issues, the less they spent with people.

Moreover, before new pastoral leaders could be trained, several of the church's founders moved away. When they left, the church lost not only an extensive reservoir of ministry skills, but also respected pastoral leaders who clearly understood why God had called Trinity into being.

As the burden on the elders increased, they responded to

various needs and requests as effectively as possible. The elders approved just about any request made by the congregation as long as the church could pay for it and enough people requested it. Before long, Trinity had a number of marginally fruitful programs that were draining significant human and financial resources. One elder reflected, "A lot was going on, but much of it had nothing to do with the church's basic mission."

BENEFITS OF CLEARLY ESTABLISHING AND EMPHASIZING THE CHURCH'S MISSION

The confusion and discouragement Trinity experienced could have been avoided. Firmly establishing and clearly emphasizing the church's mission could have helped the church stay on course. This is true for any church. A clear sense of purpose is essential. It is a constant reminder to pastoral leaders of why the church exists at all.[1] As discussed at length below, the primary purpose of the church is not to provide coffee and doughnuts for international students on Saturday mornings. That may be one way to accomplish one key aspect of the church's mission (evangelism), but one should not confuse means (providing doughnuts) with ends (evangelism).

Second, clearly articulating the church's mission helps to define what members of the body will or will not do. Once the pastoral leaders at Trinity concluded that providing coffee and doughnuts for international students on Saturday morning was not appreciated and did not facilitate their developing relationships with students, they dropped it.

A clear understanding of their mission also helped the leaders at Trinity to avoid getting involved in bingo as a way to raise money. They decided that it was a questionable activity that would undermine the credibility of their witness in the community.

A third benefit of clearly expressing the church's mission is that it helps the congregation to focus on the particular needs God has called them to address. For example, the consensus of the body at Trinity was that God had called them to have a special ministry to college students.

THE MISSION OF THE LOCAL CHURCH

To accomplish God's call to the church, pastoral leaders must answer two basic questions:

1. What is the purpose of the church?
2. To whom has God called this church to minister?

The answers to these two questions will vary according to a church's special history, traditions, location, the needs of the community, and the working of God in the lives of the people. Nevertheless, most pastoral leaders would agree that Scripture sets forth three basic purposes of the church.[2] (See figure 4-1.)

Worship

Ray Stedman of Peninsula Bible Church of Palo Alto, California, wrote that "the first aim of the church is to live to the praise and glory of God."[3] In this statement he was faithfully affirming what the apostle Paul expressed repeatedly in the book of Ephesians: We have been predestined to become God's children to praise and glorify him (Ephesians 1:6, 12, 14).

Although Scripture does not give a definition of "worship," the word means "to attribute worth,"[4] and a number of terms are used to describe its nature. For example *proskuneō* denotes an act of bowing to show reverence (Matthew 4:9; John 4:21, 23).[5] The word *sebomai* stresses the idea of "a reverent attitude" (Matthew 15:19; 2 Peter 1:3).[6] The word *latreuō* is frequently translated "service" and is used to denote "the carrying out of religious duties" (Romans 12:1; 2 Timothy 1:3).[7] *Doxazō* means to "praise, honor, magnify" (Matthew 5:16; 1 Corinthians 10:31).[8] In summary, worship involves a response to God whereby we declare his worth because of who he is and what he has done.[9]

The manner in which a church fulfills its primary purpose of worship may vary considerably. Some churches have very formal church services and sing only traditional hymns. The church I attend uses a lot of contemporary music and has a very informal worship service. Churches may have different styles, but most have many commonalities—the reading of Scripture, teaching, music, prayer, Communion. Style of worship is to some extent arbitrary and negotiable. What cannot be tampered with, however, is God's desire for us to worship him in all that we do. Moreover, worship is not restricted to Sunday. As Paul said, "Whether you eat or drink or whatever you do, do all for the glory of God" (1 Corinthians 10:31).

Edification

Because God desires the church to worship him and reflect his glory in the world, it is to be expected that he has provided a means whereby believers can be strengthened and enabled to accomplish their task. In Ephesians 4:8–16 Paul explains that God has given gifted men and women to the church for the purpose of equipping the saints to minister to one another so that the church can be "edi/ "built up," and "spiritually strengthened."[10] Jesus referred to the same process when he instructed his disciples to teach men to "observe" what he had taught them (Matthew 28:19–20).

The process by which believers can be "built up" and trained to minister to one another will be discussed at length in the next chapter. At this point I simply note that the Holy Spirit provides believers with unlimited resources (Ephesians 3:16–20) whereby they can grow and mature in Christ (Colossians 1:28–29). No book, no professor, and no seminary can ever surpass what God can accomplish and is accomplishing in building his body. It is, after all, a royal priesthood (1 Peter 2:5).

Figure 4-1
The Mission of the Local Church

	Worship	Edification	Evangelism
Christ	Deuteronomy 6:13 Matthew 4:10 John 4:19–24	Matthew 28:19–20 John 15	Matthew 4:19 Matthew 28:19–20 John 20:21 Acts 1:8
Paul	Romans 12:1–2 1 Corinthians 10:31 Ephesians 1:6 Ephesians 1:12, 14 Ephesians 3:21 1 Timothy 1:17	Ephesians 4:1–30 2 Timothy 2:2	2 Corinthians 5:18–20 Ephesians 3:1–13 Philippians 1:5
Peter	1 Peter 1:7 1 Peter 2:5, 9	1 Peter 1:22 1 Peter 2:2, 9 1 Peter 4:10 1 Peter 5:1–4	1 Peter 2:9–12 1 Peter 3:15

Evangelism

The word "evangelism" means "to bring or announce the good news."[11] What good news? That Christ has died for sin and provided salvation for all who believe (John 3:16). Proclaiming the gospel is such a major emphasis of Scripture that it seems impossible to miss it. Yet, when a church is growing and a body's needs for edification are mushrooming, it is very easy for the church to focus on itself and neglect those outside the church.

In a compelling book entitled *The Pastor-Evangelist*, Roger S. Greenway states that the separation in theory and practice between pastoral work and evangelism is one of the chief sources of the church's weakness and the explanation why many churches do not grow.[12] Greenway identifies this as a flaw that transcends denominational, theological, and cultural traditions. Scripture repeatedly shows how Jesus, Paul, Peter, and other early church leaders consistently blended evangelism and pastoral care as they discharged their duties (Acts 9:32–43; 20:19–38). Isn't that what the parable of the lost sheep is all about (Matthew 18:12–14; Luke 15:4–7)? Dare we neglect such a vital function of the church?

How pastoral leaders discharge their evangelistic responsibilities will differ according to their gifts and personalities, but it is a mandate that everyone must understand and be committed to. Moreover, it will require pastoral leaders to provide scriptural teaching on the importance of evangelism, practical training in how to do it, and modeling of it in their own lives and ministries.

CREATIVITY, BALANCE, AND OVERLAP

Every church is unique. Therefore the expression of each church's divinely ordained mission can vary dramatically from that of other churches (fig. 4-2). For example, the church I attend (Fellowship Bible Church of Park Cities) uses three words to express its mission: celebration, caring, and communication.

Celebration corresponds with worship and underscores the importance of "responding to God's grace and truth." Caring, which corresponds with edification, is used to emphasize the church's commitment to "promoting the growth and health of Christ's body." Communication corresponds with evangelism and involves "sharing God's good news with the world."

The terms a church uses to communicate its mission are important, but maintaining a healthy balance in all the segments of the mission is really crucial. For example, many churches emphasize Sunday morning worship services but neglect edification and evangelism. I am of the opinion that several of the leading evangelical churches in Dallas focus too much on edification to the neglect of evangelism at home and abroad.

Figure 4-2
Expressions of Mission

	FBC–PC	Crossroads Community	Chapel Hill Bible Church
Worship	Celebration	Praise	Exaltation
Edification	Caring	Prepare Provide	Edification
Evangelism	Communication	Proclamation	Evangelism

Fellowship Bible Church–Park Cities is in Dallas, Texas.
Crossroads Community Church is in Camarillo, California.
Chapel Hill Bible Church is in Chapel Hill, North Carolina.

An assortment of factors causes a church to overemphasize certain aspects of its mission to the detriment of others. Quite often a congregation will unconsciously adopt the characteristics of its pastor if he has a strong personality. If he is excited about evangelism, the church and its ministries will sooner or later reflect his enthusiasm. But if he is not personally committed to evangelism, the church may not fulfill its charge in that regard. The only way to prevent an imbalance from developing is for the church to review the major aspects of its mission continually and for all members of the body to take part in its fulfillment.

Crossroads Community Church developed a mission statement that cogently blends the three-pronged purpose of the church (fig. 4-3). These interlocking purposes provide a stable and godly vision to shape the future of this church.

Finally, it is important to remember that the three major aspects of the church's mission overlap with one another considerably. For example, the primary purpose of congregational singing may be to worship God, but believers are certainly edified in the process, and nonbelievers may actually come to know the Lord through the ministry of music. The apostle Paul essentially said this with respect to "prophesying" in church meetings; specifically, nonbelievers may come to know the Lord through exhortations from Scripture (1 Corinthians 14:20–25).

44

Figure 4-3
Mission Statement
Crossroads Community Church

WE EXIST TO PRAISE GOD . . .

through celebrating new life in Jesus.
through responding to His presence in our lives.
through allowing His Holy Spirit to lead us.

Praise is our way of expressing our deep love for God.
In worship we submit to His lordship in our lives and reflect His
majesty, glory, and power.

PREPARE OURSELVES FOR SERVICE . . .

through the study and application of Scripture.
through developing our talents and spiritual gifts.
through becoming mature in Jesus Christ.

Preparation and growth is vital. It is not merely an option. However,
growth is not an end in itself. Therefore, we seek to grow and become mature so that we can be prepared for service to our Lord,
Jesus Christ.

PROVIDE LOVE AND CARE FOR ONE ANOTHER . . .

through sharing each others needs, burdens, and joys.
through serving each other in a sacrificial way.
through learning how to love and be loved.

God, in His grace, has given us to each other. An integral part of
our life as His body is caring for and supporting each other.

PROCLAIM CHRIST TO THE WORLD

through the penetration of our society.
through reproducing ourselves by evangelism and discipleship.
through applying ourselves and our resources in reaching out to our
community, our nation and our world.

We take seriously our Lord's command to go and make disciples.
Mission is the bedrock of our reason for being.

KNOW THY NICHE

One of the hidden benefits of an economic recession and
the accompanying decline in donations is that it tends to force
churches (and other nonprofit organizations) to tighten their

belts and focus on their basic mission. In the absence of external forces like a recession, however, a surprising number of organizations allow programs to proliferate without carefully evaluating their relationship to the organization's mission.

Although Trinity was not affected by an economic recession, the spiritual recession that hit the remnant on the elder board had a similar effect. It caused them to regroup and return to the basics. Besides reconfirming their commitment to the basic purposes of the church, the elders also clarified their thinking with respect to whom God had called them to minister.

ALL THINGS TO ALL PEOPLE?

As mentioned earlier, when the church was first established, the elders believed God had called them to have a special ministry to college students. During the church's boom years, however, a lot of programs were initiated that had little support, rendering them ineffective. Sometimes the programs were initiated by the elders or staff; with others, interested members of the body took the initiative. Quite often they were identical to programs that were already being sponsored by other churches (such as Mother's Day Out or Meals on Wheels).

But a church cannot be "all things to all people." That is why it is important to "know thy niche," to stand back from the action and ask, "Are we being faithful to our calling? Are we functioning like a spiritual community—or a religious cafeteria that is trying to provide something for everyone?"

After prayerfully rethinking their basic mission, the elders at Trinity concluded that for the present time and the near future, the Lord had called them to focus their efforts on three major groups: (1) college students, (2) young families and their children, and (3) missionaries and their fields. Everyone was welcome at Trinity, but the elders recognized that some people with special needs could be ministered to more effectively elsewhere. University Presbyterian Church was better equipped to minister to senior citizens and shut-ins. The Methodist Church had an excellent Mother's Day Out program. Unless God clearly directed them to do so, it didn't make sense for Trinity to try to duplicate these efforts.

Target-Grouping

In his book *The Church Unleashed*, Frank Tillapaugh, pastor of Bear Valley Baptist Church in Denver, explains how to design special ministries to meet the needs of often neglected subgroups in society.[13] His concept of a target group can be equated with the three groups mentioned above. Once the body senses the Lord's leading them to minister to a certain group (such as college students), the pastoral leaders of that project need to study the specific needs of the target group and devise a strategy for meeting those needs.

The process used at Bear Valley Baptist Church enables pastoral leaders to define to whom God has called them to minister, a question churches seldom consider. The questioning is essential. The Lord himself engaged in a similar process when he chose twelve men to be with him for special training. He continued to minister to the multitudes, but he focused on twelve men to accomplish his mission. The results are history.

NOTES

1. Edward R. Dayton, and Ted W. Engstrom, "Defining the Mission," *Christian Leadership Letter* (June 1984): 1–3.
2. Alvin J. Lindgren, *Management For Your Church: A Systems Approach* (Nashville: Abingdon, 1981), 50–52.
3. Ray Stedman, *Body Life* (Glendale, Calif.: Regal, 1972).
4. Robert L. Saucy, *The Church in God's Program* (Chicago: Moody, 1972), 166–68.
5. Walter Bauer, *A Greek-English Lexicon of the New Testament and Other Early Christian Literature*, trans. W. F. Arndt and F. W. Gingrich (Chicago: University of Chicago Press, 1957), 723–24.
6. Ibid., 753.
7. Ibid., 468.

8. Ibid., 202–3.

9. Robert Webber, *Worship Is a Verb* (Waco, Tex.: Word, 1985), 28–30.

10. Bauer, *A Greek-English Lexicon of the New Testament*, 560–61.

11. Ibid., 317.

12. Roger S. Greenway, ed., *The Pastor-Evangelist: Preacher, Model, and Mobilizer for Church Growth* (Phillipsburg, N.J.: Presbyterian and Reformed, 1987), 1–14.

13. Frank Tillapaugh, *The Church Unleashed* (Ventura, Calif.: Regal, 1982).

Chapter 5

Equipping: Enabling Members of the Body to Minister

And He gave some as apostles, and some as prophets, and some as evangelists, and some as pastors and teachers, for the equipping of the saints for the work of service, to the building up of the body of Christ.

(Ephesians 4:11–12 NASB)

Whatever titles we give leaders in churches today . . . their common mission is an equipping one.

Larry Richards
A Theology of Church Leadership

Shortly after I became a Christian, I joined a Bible study and met someone who began to teach me how to pray, memorize Scripture, study the Bible, and share my faith. Later on, when I enrolled at the University of North Carolina, the same person challenged me to get involved in a campus ministry, taught me how to lead small group Bible studies, and showed me how to encourage others.

Bill Rapier and I have always felt that God gave us a special Paul–Timothy relationship, but I don't think I fully appreciated how significantly God had used him in my life until after I graduated from seminary and became an elder in the local church. As much as I value my seminary education, Bill taught me far more about developing my relationship with God and ministering to others than most of my seminary professors.

The fruitful friendship Bill and I shared is not unlike the mentor relationships in the business world. These close, trusted advisory relationships are rare in corporations and, unfortunately, just as rare in the church. Since one of the primary functions of pastoral leaders is to equip members of the body for ministry (service), the need is intense for encouraging honest confidants. The absence of these invaluable dynamics leaves a large gap in the church.

WHAT IS EQUIPPING?

To grasp fully the biblical concept of equipping, it is important to keep in mind Paul's description of the church as the body of Christ.

The word "equip" derives from the Greek noun *katartismos*, a medical term for "the setting of a broken bone." It also means "preparation."[1] "To equip is to put a bone or a part of the human body into right relationship with the other parts of the body so that every part fits thoroughly."[2]

The verb form, *katartizō*, is used thirteen times in the New Testament and means "to put in order, to restore, to put in proper condition, to make complete."[3] For example, the benediction to the book of Hebrews says that the Good Shepherd (Jesus) will "equip you with every good thing for doing his will" (Hebrews 13:20–21). The basic idea being developed is that Christ makes it possible for (that is, enables) believers to do his will.

Paul makes similar use of the term *katartizō* in Ephesians 4:12, where he writes that God has given members of the body gifts "to prepare God's people for works of service."[4] In short, one of the major responsibilities of pastoral leaders is to train/enable church members to minister to one another.

WHY IS EQUIPPING IMPORTANT?

We must ultimately recognize that failing to equip members of the body for ministry is disobedience to God. Negligence in this matter also has practical consequences: pastoral leaders become weary. That was certainly the case at Trinity. When some of the founding elders moved away, those remaining assumed more responsibility than they could handle. It is no wonder some of the elders did not find their roles spiritually rewarding. Taking on more responsibility than one should for an extended period of time, even under the best of circumstances, can cripple anyone after a while. The symptoms of "battle fatigue" are obvious. Besides feeling physically and emotionally worn out, there is a loss of creativity and joy.

Failing to equip members of the body for ministry also acts as a constraint on individual and corporate growth. Peter Wagner has pointed out, "Most of the things God does in the world are done through Christians who are working together in community, complementing each other with their gifts in their local congregations."[5] In other words, for a spiritual community to grow, pastoral leaders must (1) help church members understand their spiritual gifts and personal responsibility to minister, and (2) encourage them to use their spiritual gifts in practical ministry.

Trinity's elders firmly believed that participating in small groups such as Bible studies, discipleship groups, and fellowship groups was a valuable, catalyst to spiritual growth and maturity. Ironically, when the demand for small groups increased, there weren't enough "equipped" group leaders. As a result many people missed the growth opportunities that come from ministering and developing close relationships

51

with other believers in small groups. The net effect was that the body did not grow as much as it might have.

It is also important to equip members of the body for service so that opportunities to minister to those outside the church are not missed. One of the saddest facets of Trinity's struggles is that it was not ready to respond to some of the very needs the elders felt God had called them to meet. For example, although several international students visited the church, few people were prepared to minister to them. Moreover, many of the young college students who wanted to be involved in the church joined campus ministries instead, simply because the church was not ready to provide the nurturing and ministry opportunities they needed.

Why is equipping essential? Without it, the church cannot accomplish its mission.

THE DIFFICULTY OF EQUIPPING OTHERS TO MINISTER

At this point, some readers may be thinking, "If equipping members of the body for ministry is so important, why is it seldom done?"

That is a simple question with a complex answer. To begin with, determining how to help believers discover and use their spiritual gifts is difficult and time-consuming. This was one of the major conclusions drawn from a *Leadership* survey done a few years ago. More than 70 percent of the pastors interviewed indicated that they needed good training programs but did not have time to develop them.[6] It appears that when a church most needs solid training for leaders (that is, when it is growing rapidly), there is less time available for equipping the saints.

Another roadblock to equipping members of the body for ministry is pastors who fear that they will lose their status and power in the church. Frank Tillapaugh goes so far as to say that "the pastor is the key to developing lay leaders."[7] Tillapaugh is probably right, for in spite of all the gains made by the church renewal movement in recent years, in most churches laypeople are still very dependent on "full-time Christian workers." In other words, when it comes to real-life ministry, the clergy are regarded as the professionals; the laity are the amateurs. Although I wish the terms "laity" and "clergy" would disappear, it is unlikely to happen because they are solidly entrenched in American religious culture. We can hope that the imbalance in their status and roles will gradually be corrected.

Undeniably, the senior pastor and other staff members, by virtue of their education, responsibilities, and proximity to board members, tend to exert much influence over church affairs. Their influence, however, should not be exerted at the expense of the body. The church is, after all, a "priesthood" of believers, and the spiritual gifts of every member, not just the staff, are needed for the church to realize its full potential (1 Peter 2:9; 4:10). Peter Wagner has said, "To the degree that every member of a given congregation has discovered, developed, and is using his or her spiritual gifts, the congregation can be said to be healthy."[8]

One of the exciting aspects of Trinity is that its senior pastor had a vision for helping members of the body develop their spiritual gifts. John never wanted to function autocratically, and he did not want to "build a big church." Yet there was still something amiss within the body. This was largely due to the fact that Trinity, much like the university town in which it was located, highly valued "brain power." As long as John delivered intellectually stimulating sermons, most people assumed they were growing spiritually and were content with the status quo. They didn't see the need for using the gifts the Lord gave them.

Part of this problem is that over the years the evangelical church has been significantly influenced by the rationalism of secular society, which has its roots in Hellenistic philosophy. As a result many Christians have come to assume that an intellectual understanding of the Bible is equivalent to wisdom, knowledge, obedience, and spiritual maturity. As much as I personally value education, I agree wholeheartedly with Frank Tillapaugh when he says, "If dumping content on

53

people produced mature Christians, the church in the United States would be by far the most mature church which history has ever seen."[9]

If dumping content is *not* the way to equip the saints for ministry, what is?

ESTABLISHING A FOUNDATION FOR EQUIPPING

Happily, there are a number of ways to equip believers, especially since no two churches are the same. But pastoral leaders must both understand and be committed to the importance of equipping because the process requires a great deal of time, energy, and patience. Lloyd Jacobsen, pastor of Bethel Temple in St. Paul, has said:

> Some things in the kingdom, the really important ones, are not taught in the classroom. Rather, they are absorbed from demonstration in a variety of circumstances over a period of time, often at great personal cost to the demonstrating teacher.[10]

Recognizing that every church is unique, the following sections are intended to help you think through some of the issues that may emerge as you develop an approach to equipping. Let me underscore the need to be sensitive to the leading of the Holy Spirit and his gifts to the members of your church.

Basic Teaching

Although seldom recognized as such, teaching is one of the most important managerial functions of pastoral leaders. It is especially important when it comes to equipping members of the body for ministry, because many church members are not familiar with basic Bible doctrine and the nature and purpose of the local church. Furthermore, churches that have historically functioned like institutions will need to spend a great deal of time helping church members understand (1) the distinctiveness of the body, (2) the difference between a church community and a business corporation, and

(3) the mission of the church: worship, edification, and evangelism. Ted Ward, an education professor at Michigan State University, has said that the objective of such teaching is not to provide people with a higher level of "clarified information," but to encourage obedience and a will to act on the truth.[11] (See also Romans 6:4; 1 Corinthians 3; 1 John 1:6–7.)

Character Development

Church members need to be challenged and equipped to live godly lives. The values and priorities of the body of Christ are vastly different from the values and priorities of contemporary culture (Romans 12:1–2). Many people, such as J. Paul Stevens, author of *Liberating the Laity,* believe that equipping should be more concerned with character formation than with skills or information. There is no question that Paul underscored the importance of character qualifications for pastoral leaders (1 Timothy 3; Titus 1). Fortunately it's not an either-or situation. All three are vital: character, skills, and knowledge. This leads me to a third aspect of establishing a foundation for equipping the saints: helping people to discover and use their spiritual gifts.

Spiritual Gifts

An extensive discussion of spiritual gifts is beyond the scope of this chapter, but a few major observations are in order. Let's start with a good working definition of a spiritual gift. A spiritual gift is a special attribute or ability given by the Holy Spirit to every Christian according to God's grace for the edification of the body of Christ (Romans 12:6).

The Holy Spirit has given every Christian at least one spiritual gift according to God's grace (1 Peter 4:10). Spiritual gifts have not been reserved just for spiritual superstars. God has "gifted" each member of the body just as he pleases (1 Corinthians 12:24–25). Most people have several spiritual gifts—such as teaching—that can be developed with training and experience. Because of the intrinsic unity in the body, each member needs the other members *and* the ministry of their gifts (1 Corinthians 12:12–25). What is the purpose of spiritual gifts? They are to be used for the edification (building up) of the body of Christ (Ephesians 4:12), which glorifies God (1 Peter 4:10–11).

There is no secret formula for discovering one's spiritual gifts. Peter Wagner recommends the following process: (1) explore the possibilities, (2) experiment with exercising different gifts, (3) examine your feelings, (4) evaluate your effectiveness, and (5) expect confirmation from the body.[12] Figure 5-1, which is based on Romans 12, 1 Corinthians 12, and Ephesians 4, contains a basic overview of spiritual gifts. Neither it nor the lists of gifts from which it was culled are exhaustive. Most important is to remember that for the body to grow and reach its potential, all members need to use their spiritual gifts in service.[13]

Figure 5-1
Overview of Spiritual Gifts

1. *Administration*	The ability to provide guidance, direction, leadership, and care for the church
2. *Apostleship*	The ability to serve as a special messenger of God
3. *Discernment*	The ability to distinguish between true and false sources of revelation
4. *Evangelism*	The ability to share the gospel with unbelievers
5. *Exhortation*	The ability to encourage, comfort, and admonish other members of the body constructively
6. *Faith*	The ability to believe in God's power to meet specific needs
7. *Giving*	The ability to contribute one's material resources to other members of the body
8. *Hospitality*	The ability to provide an open house and warm welcome for those in need of food and shelter
9. *Mercy*	The ability to provide comfort, empathy, and kindness to people in distress
10. *Miracles and healing*	The ability to perform powerful acts for God and restore health apart from natural means
11. *Pastor*	The ability to lead, protect, guide, and care for other members of the body of Christ
12. *Prophecy*	The ability to understand and communicate an immediate message of God to his people

13. *Service*		The ability to identify needs and help to meet them
14. *Teaching*		The ability to understand God's revelation and communicate in a way that others are able to learn
15. *Tongues*		The ability to speak in a language one has never learned

Adapted from Charles C. Ryrie, *The Holy Spirit* (Chicago: Moody, 1965), and C. Peter Wagner, *Your Spiritual Gifts Can Help Your Church Grow* (Ventura, Calif.: Regal, 1979).

THE SCOPE OF EQUIPPING

To participate meaningfully in the life of the church and to contribute to the accomplishment of its mission, a few basic ministry skills are essential. However your church approaches the process of equipping, you will benefit by incorporating the following factors. First, all members of the body need to know how to develop their relationship with God, the head of the body. Teaching and training on the following topics pay big dividends: personal devotions, Bible study, prayer, meditation, and Scripture memory. The most valuable lesson I learned from Bill Rapier was how to develop my relationship with God. This was most significant because it set other things in motion. As J. I. Packer said, "Knowing about God is crucially important for the living of our lives."[14]

Second, all Christians need to know how to share their faith (1 Peter 3:15). This is an area in which parachurch organizations excel and most churches fail. An increasing number of pastoral leaders, such as T. M. Moore, executive pastor of ministries at Church of the Savior in Wayne, Pennsylvania, are equipping the saints "to bear effective testimony to the Lord Jesus Christ in the normal context of their everyday lives, through the formal and casual relationships in which they are involved, and in a manner and at a level that conforms to the needs and interests of their hearers."[15] As Moore explains, effective training in lifestyle evangelism requires (1) visible and effective models (1 Corinthians 4:16; Philippians 3:17), (2) opportunities to observe and develop the skill in real-life situations, (3) clear instruction on the work of the Holy Spirit in evangelistic endeavors, (4) a commitment to the long haul, and (5) realistic expectations. Conversion, in the final analysis, is God's work.

Third, members of the body need to be given an opportunity to develop some basic "body-life" ministry skills such as how to pray, teach, and share in a small group. Speaking in public and sharing personal information in a small group can be very difficult for some, but most people can gradually learn to do them. This is essential to be able to minister to one another, since it is difficult, if not impossible, to minister to someone you do not know.

THE CONTEXT FOR EQUIPPING

One of the reasons my relationship with Bill Rapier was so fruitful is that we spent a great deal of time together and I was able to learn attributes of Christianity in the natural course of life. For example, I learned how to share my faith by watching Bill talk with friends during lunch, not by taking a class on evangelism. I learned how to encourage others by watching Bill encourage others. I learned how to study the Bible by searching the Scriptures in my parents' living room with Bill, a Bible, and a list of questions.

The individual attention or "one-on-one" time Bill and I shared is not often feasible except in college or military ministries that deal primarily with singles, but it is possible to nurture similar equipping relationships in small groups. For example, Fellowship Bible Church of Park Cities in Dallas regularly sponsors discipleship groups designed to cultivate many of the basic ministry skills mentioned above. The groups consist of ten to fifteen church members who meet weekly for three to six months. Each member is responsible for leading a different part of the meeting (Bible study, prayer, or sharing). Group leaders work hard to create and maintain a nonthreatening atmosphere to allow people freedom to learn how to minister without embarrassment or fear of rejection. Group members also read and discuss books and articles that deal with leadership and group dynamics.

Whether done individually or in small groups, providing members of the body with opportunities to develop their spiritual gifts and ministry skills is an important equipping function of pastoral leaders. And though I am deeply grateful for the fruitfulness of parachurch organizations, I am firmly convinced that the local church, with its natural networks, diversity of gifts, and unity in Christ, is the best environment for developing practical ministry skills.

The challenge for pastoral leaders is (1) to encourage others to use their spiritual gifts, and (2) to provide opportunities for ministry skills development. It is essential that pastoral leaders take into account that each member of the body has unique gifts and cannot be squeezed into some predetermined mold. In addition, pastoral leaders need to remember that their primary responsibility is not to do all the work of the ministry themselves, but "to restore and prepare" others for ministry.[16]

A TIMELESS CHALLENGE

It is tempting to think that the church's growing awareness of the need to equip the saints is strictly a recent phenomenon. But some forty years ago, Henry C. Theissen, professor of systematic theology at Wheaton College, commenting on the purpose of the church and its need to edify and educate its members, wrote, "Many local churches have been entirely too slow to see the need of such training."[17]

No, the "need" isn't new, and equipping still requires making sacrifices. But it's worth the effort! For when pastoral leaders grasp the significance of spiritual gifts, equipping, and body life, they invariably begin to function less like CEOs and more like servant-leaders who assist others in developing their skills and abilities (Mark 10:45). Then when members of the body risk involvement in "frontline" ministry, they further their own growth and enable the church to accomplish its mission.[18]

NOTES

1. Colin Brown, ed., *The New International Dictionary of New Testament Theology*, 3 vols. (Grand Rapids: Zondervan, 1975), 1:302.

2. J. Paul Stevens, *Liberating the Laity* (Downers Grove, Ill.: InterVarsity, 1985), 25.

3. Walter Bauer, *A Greek-English Lexicon of the New Testament and Other Early Christian Literature*, trans. W. F. Arndt and F. W. Gingrich (Chicago: University of Chicago Press, 1957), 418–19.

4. Ibid., 418.

5. C. Peter Wagner, *Your Spiritual Gifts Can Help Your Church Grow* (Ventura, Calif.: Regal, 1979), 44.

6. Terry C. Muck, "Training Volunteers: A Leadership Survey," *Leadership* (Summer 1982): 40–48.

7. Frank Tillapaugh, *The Church Unleashed* (Ventura, Calif.: Regal, 1982), 106.

8. C. Peter Wagner, "Good Pastors Don't Make Churches Grow," *Leadership* (Winter 1981): 71.

9. Tillapaugh, *The Church Unleashed*, 134.

10. LLoyd Jacobsen, "Who Decides What Deacons Do?" *Leadership* (Summer 1983): 67–71.

11. Ted W. Ward, "Evaluating Metaphors of Education," *Bibliotheca Sacra* (October–December 1982): 291–301.

12. Wagner, *Your Spiritual Gifts*, 116.

13. Charles C. Ryrie, *The Holy Spirit* (Chicago: Moody, 1965), 83–92.

14. J. I. Packer, *Knowing God* (Downers Grove, Ill.: InterVarsity, 1975), 14.

15. Roger S. Greenway, ed., *The Pastor-Evangelist: Preacher, Model, and Mobilizer for Church Growth* (Phillipsburg, N.J.: Presbyterian and Reformed, 1987), 130–39.

16. *The Compact Edition of the Oxford English Dictionary*, vol. 1 (New York: Oxford, 1971), 258.

17. Henry C. Theissen, *Introductory Lectures in Systematic Theology* (Grand Rapids: Eerdmans, 1949), 432–35.

18. Larry Richards and Clyde Hoeldtke, *A Theology of Church Leadership* (Grand Rapids: Zondervan, 1982), 92.

Chapter 6

Relationships: Reflecting the Spirit of the Lord

And so, as those who have been chosen of God, holy and beloved, put on a heart of compassion, kindness, humility, gentleness and patience;

Bearing with one another, and forgiving each other, whoever has a complaint against anyone; just as the Lord forgave you, so also should you.

And beyond all these things put on love, which is the perfect bond of unity. (Colossians 3:12–14 NASB)

During the summer following my junior year in college, I was blessed with an opportunity to go backpacking in Europe and spent a week at L'Abri. Although I was a relatively new Christian, I had become a serious student of the Bible and enjoyed lively theological discussions. Besides, I had never been to Switzerland, and in the early seventies, going to L'Abri was the "in" thing.

My youthful naïveté notwithstanding, I left L'Abri a changed person. It was not because I met Francis Schaeffer (he was out of town). Nor was it because I resolved some personally troubling philosophical issue (I try not to let philosophy ever bother me). Frankly, I did not even participate in any lively theological discussions.

What did impress me, however, was the quality of relationships among believers living at L'Abri. Even now it is difficult to explain, but their love for one another and kindness to wandering students like me, who had a penchant for dropping in unannounced, was overpowering.

Up to that time, I had focused my energies on developing my "personal" relationship with God and was engrossed in duties to sustain my walk with the Lord (that is, personal devotions, memorizing Scripture, Bible study). At L'Abri, however, I began to understand the importance of cultivating my relationships with other members of the body of Christ. One passage of Scripture that especially came to life for me that week was Colossians 3.

Although I had read it several times and had enjoyed some precious fellowship with other Christians before going to Europe, at L'Abri I began to understand more fully the primacy of loving and living in unity with other believers. I realized that the church is an organism, of which Christ is the head, and that we are members of his body (Romans 12:5; Ephesians 4:15). Inasmuch as the church expresses his character in the contemporary world, we are continuing his incarnation. Paul told the Corinthians, "You are a letter of Christ . . . written not with ink, but with the Spirit of the living God" (2 Corinthians 3:2–4).

I have long forgotten the names of the people I met at L'Abri, but I still remember their love for one another and their hospitality to strangers. Moreover, having served as a church elder for several years, I have become increasingly convinced that developing and maintaining quality relationships in the church is a major shepherding responsibility of pastoral leaders and a key to the church being able to accomplish its mission.[1]

RELATIONSHIPS AND THE MISSION
OF THE CHURCH

Evangelism

When I was in college, there were two predominant approaches to witnessing on campus: friendship evangelism, and a method euphemistically referred to as "cold turkey." Both incorporated a clear presentation of the gospel, but similarities ended there.

People who preferred friendship evangelism were usually more easy-going and casual in their approach than the cold-turkey champions. They worked hard at developing relationships with people before attempting to share the gospel, and they enjoyed friendly dialogue.

Advocates of the cold-turkey method (who outnumbered the proponents of friendship evangelism three to one) were more aggressive. They frequently went door-to-door through dormitories on campus, sharing the gospel with anyone who would listen. They even followed one of my suitemates into the shower room (how's that for persistence?). They usually used tracts like "The Four Spiritual Laws," and they invariably pressed for an immediate "decision."

I would never recommend following anybody into the shower, but there is certainly room for a variety of approaches in sharing the gospel. I personally prefer friendship (also called "lifestyle") evangelism. It is better suited to my temperament and spiritual gifts. Although it is often criticized for being too low-key, friendship evangelism has become more popular than "cold turkey" in recent years and in some studies has been shown to be more effective.

For example, in a recent study of 240 Christians, about 70 percent of those still active in their churches indicated they came to know Christ through a person who put a priority on developing a genuine relationship with them.[2]

In contrast, 87 percent of those no longer active in a church described the approach to evangelism by which they were converted as being "manipulative monologue." (That is, unfortunately, characteristic of the cold-turkey approach.)

Discussing this point further in *The Master's Plan for Making Disciples*, Win Arn persuasively shows that building and strengthening relationships with non-Christians is a more honest and effective approach to evangelism because it demonstrates a genuine concern for the whole person.[3]

EDIFICATION

One of the basic premises underlying this book is that, for the body of Christ to grow, believers must use their spiritual gifts in mutual ministry. I know that sounds simple and logical. After all, how can you minister to someone unless you have a relationship with that person? It is difficult, at best, because you cannot know what a person's real needs are or what they will respond to unless you spend time getting to know the individual. Each of us is unique. That is why pastoral leaders must develop relationships with the people to whom God has called them to minister. As they model healthy relationships, others in the church will begin forming their own networks.

Unfortunately, many evangelical Christians still think that listening to dynamic speakers ad infinitum and memorizing doctrine are the keys to spiritual growth. Ministering to others and being ministered to by others in the body of Christ are seen as secondary. We must remember, however, that understanding content does not produce Christian maturity.[4] In actuality, no church can afford to let an overemphasis on teaching lead to a neglect of fellowship and personal ministry. Indeed, relationships are essential to individual and corporate growth in the body!

Worship

One characteristic of L'Abri that impressed me most was the simplicity and the sincerity of worship. Neither the chapel nor the music was overpowering, but there was a refreshing responsiveness to God because of who he was and what he was doing. This created a sense of expectancy when we gathered together as a family to sing hymns and pray.

WHY CHURCH RELATIONSHIPS SOMETIMES LANGUISH

As committed as I am to the importance of developing and maintaining quality relationships in the church, I know that problems develop even under the best circumstances. Quite often it is simply due to the almost universal idealism many Christians bring to the church. Keith Huttenlocker explains this in his excellent book *Becoming the Family of God:* "Most of us expect our local congregation to be a kind of spiritual Camelot, where every man is a Dale Carnegie graduate, and every woman is a candidate for the Miss Congeniality award."[5]

The truth, of course, is that every church is made up of imperfect people like you and me, some of whom we might not have chosen for membership if it had been left to us. Yes, they are "precious in His sight," and "blessed with every spiritual blessing in the heavenly places in Christ," but at times they are also late for meetings, difficult to understand, and insensitive. When the bubble finally pops, it is tempting to withdraw and keep our distance, which only leads to further disillusionment and alienation. As John White says beautifully in *The Fight,* "When Christ demands you commit yourself to an enduring responsibility toward people you may not naturally care for, he is really doing you a favor. He is insisting that you facilitate the very thing you need, a caring community whose members never fail one another."[6]

Another reason why relationships sometimes languish in the local church is that many Christians fail to realize that developing good relationships takes time and requires that people honestly face one another. As anyone who has worked at it knows, good relationships do not just "happen." They have to be carefully nurtured.[7] Unfortunately, we live in a transient and results-oriented society that demands quick results and does not appreciate the value of long-term relationships. This is especially problematic in big cities like Dallas with an abundance of good churches. I know a lot of people who select church services like dishes at a restaurant.

When the "menu" no longer suits their taste, they sample elsewhere.

Another factor muddying the waters of honest relationships is that churches tend to emphasize a problem-free life in Christ. Bruce Larson, author of the *Relational Revolution,* wrote:

> The church, unfortunately, has become a museum to display the victorious life. We keep spotlighting people who say, "I've got it made. I used to be terrible, but then I met Jesus, got zapped by the Spirit, got into a small group, got the gifts and fruits of the Holy Spirit" . . . and the implication is that they are sinners emeritus. . . . What we need in the church are models who fail because most of us fail more than we succeed.[8]

Another factor which prevents many churches from realizing growth through relationships is the average person's abhorrence of conflict, usually grounded in the fear of rejection. This is less common in corporations than in the church, where differences are frequently seen as a work of Satan and a sign of disunity. The problem, of course, is that such a mentality suppresses honest communication and stifles the growth that occurs as a result of working through differences. But this only produces a false sense of unity. It looks good on the outside, but it is hollow inside.

This particular problem began to plague Trinity as soon as new people joined the board of elders. The new elders were more open to new approaches to ministry and were much more comfortable dealing with conflict. Older board members tended to think alike and were not at all comfortable with conflict. Naturally the younger members often felt stymied and misunderstood.

An extensive discussion of conflict and resolution is beyond the scope of this book, but pastoral leaders should not be threatened by conflict or take it personally when it erupts in the church. Lynn Buzzard of the Christian Legal Society, who was formerly a pastor, has said, "A certain level of ongoing conflict or tension probably ought to be part of the church . . . if it is attempting anything important, and if anybody has strong feelings about that." For that matter, the disciples were always arguing and fussing. That is one of the reasons the Jerusalem Council was convened: to resolve some major differences in opinion (Acts 15).[9]

Another reason church relationships sometimes fail to blossom is that many people do not understand the biblical view of the church and the stress it places on relationships in the community. "The church is," Philip Yancey says, "an ideal place for nurturing relationships."[10] The problem is that a lot of American Christians are still plagued with a Lone Ranger mentality regarding church involvement. They either do not understand how the body is supposed to function or they are unwilling to surrender their independence and accept their rightful place in the family.

THE ROLE OF PASTORAL LEADERS

In most churches, pastoral leaders set the tone for the quality and depth of relationships among church members. How? By precept and practice. As I mentioned earlier, this was an area in which Trinity's senior pastor struggled. Although John was committed to the importance of relationships and frequently taught on the subject, it was difficult for him to relate to people on a personal level. He refused, however, to let people put him on a pedestal, and in the pulpit he freely acknowledged that he is human and has problems just like everyone else. In addition to his honesty, John's other saving grace was his warm and caring spirit. He was also blessed with staff members who compensated for his weak interpersonal skills.

The difficulty that John and other clergy encounter in pastoral relationships is attributable to a number of factors. One of the biggest culprits however, is the nature of their seminary education, which is highly academic and deficient in practical ministry skills training. In a study of sixty-six parish ministers, Henry Virkler showed that no amount of content-oriented theological education can give pastoral leaders the process-interpersonal skills they need to minister effectively.[11] The issue is receiving greater attention, but most seminary programs still tend to be very academic and content-oriented.

The irony, of course, if that although the apostle Paul was a first-rate scholar, he repeatedly emphasized the importance of relationships in the body of Christ. In fact, in his major list of qualifications for leadership in the local church the following are included: "gentle," "neither pugnacious" nor "contentious" (1 Timothy 3:3 NASB).

In spite of Paul's emphasis, the nature of a person's people skills remains one of the least discussed qualifications for pastoral leaders. I knew several brilliant fellows in seminary who did very well academically but have yet to develop significant pastoral ministries, largely because of their inability to relate to people.

In contrast, I have several friends who have had little "formal" theological training, but have tremendous ministries based largely upon their good relationship with the Lord, and their ability to relate well to people. In short, they are sensitive shepherds of the flock.

Developing relationships in the church that reflect Christ's love (John 13:34–35) is not "Mission Impossible." Yet Larry Richard states that to have these, a church must be characterized by the following:

1. Deep involvement in one another's life, sharing of concerns, caring, supporting, and encouraging;
2. Each person's seeking to minister to and help others in every way he can;
3. Honesty and self-revelation in all ministry situations; and
4. Commitment of each Christian to others' needs.[12]

How do pastoral leaders set the tone for relationships in the church? By setting an example. By teaching on the subject. And by encouraging others in this area.

SMALL GROUPS

In addition to personally modeling good relationships, pastoral leaders can enhance the relational quality of life in their congregations by nurturing networks of small groups. Although Trinity had problems coping with their rapid growth (which will be discussed later), the commitment of pastoral leaders to small-group ministries was one of the church's foundational strengths. Indeed, most of the elders at Trinity either led or participated in some type of small group. Everyone in the body was encouraged to find their niche in a small group. Groups varied, but most were designed to provide an opportunity for fellowship, ministry, and spiritual growth.

During the week I stayed at L'Abri, I participated in three small-group meetings consisting of Bible study, prayer, and personal sharing. I was so profoundly affected by the experience that I have been in a small group of one form or other ever since. In fact, the church I now attend has more than sixty small groups, which is one of the reasons it has been able to maintain a sense of community long after passing the 500-member mark.

BUILDING A SENSE OF COMMUNITY
AT THE CORPORATE LEVEL

When I was growing up, people used to tease my parents about being Catholic because we had five boys (plus a dog and a cat). Though my parents are not Catholic, we did have a fairly large family—huge by today's standards. More important than its size, however, was that we were close and had a lot of fun. I can still see my mother walking around saying, "Never a dull moment."

Now that my brothers and I have left home and are developing our own families, we are beginning to understand the effort our parents put into building our sense of family unity. It is staggering to think of all we took for granted: birthday parties, family vacations, trips to the beach, working around the house; all gave us a special sense of belonging, togetherness, and family.

So what has this got to do with relationships and building a sense of community in the local church? A great deal, Keith

Huttenlocker says, because it takes more than meeting together two or three times a week and quickly smoothing over disagreements for any local congregation to be one big happy family. At a minimum, building a sense of community requires celebration, tradition, and recreation.[13]

Celebrations

According to my calculations, by the time my brothers and I were on our own, my mother had planned over 115 birthday parties (seventeen of them were mine). That's a lot of celebrating. It was a lot of work for my mom, but events like that made all of us feel unique and reminded us that we were cared for by other family members.

The early church also celebrated often. In fact, they celebrated the death and resurrection of Christ every week (1 Corinthians 14). Many churches regularly celebrate marriages, births, baptisms, conversions, and confirmation. The problem is that (1) the celebrations tend to be too few and far in between, and (2) they tend to be down played—especially in conservative nondenominational churches.

There are other events a congregation can celebrate, such as the anniversary of the church's founding or special events like the completion of a building program.

Traditions

I was raised in a military family, so it is not surprising that we had plenty of traditions. For example, we never failed to watch the Army-Navy game (Go Army!). We always went to the Main Post Chapel on Christmas Eve. We always fixed Mom breakfast in bed on Mother's Day. And on many afternoons, when my dad came home from work, we would take our German shepherd for a run in the woods near our house. These were activities in which everyone could participate, and because they were fun, we did not have to worry about them being burdensome.

A church tradition does not have to be something "super-sacred"; it can be any meaningful experience valued and enjoyed by church members. No two churches will have identical traditions.

Here are some examples. They are presented not to be replicated, necessarily, but to illustrate a variety of ways to celebrate. The goal is to "brainstorm" to give you ideas for your own church.

The women in our church have a special tea every year when they gather to trim the church's Christmas tree in the sanctuary. It is by far one of the most popular and enjoyable events of the year.

The Singles Class has a big sit-down Thanksgiving dinner on the Sunday night before Thanksgiving. Members of the class spend hours cooking, arranging tables, and making decorations. It is open to all the singles in the church and provides a special family feeling for those unable to go home for the holidays.

The Missions Committee sponsors a church-wide banquet once a year to draw the church together for an in-depth focus on world missions. It is the only time during the year when the entire church can share a meal together.

Recreation

Once a year, the members of my small group go on a retreat, which usually requires driving one to two hours and spending the night in a motel. The week before we leave, I invariably question the value of it. After all, we see each other almost every other week—and retreats can be expensive!

Just as predictably, God always blesses our time together and renews the relationships within our group. One of the reasons it is such a special time is that we do a lot of different things together, like playing football, going out to eat, watching a movie, and just sitting around talking. In short, we have a lot of fun.

Our church also sponsors a number of church-wide retreats throughout the year to give members of the church an opportunity to be refreshed spiritually and to build relationships. Most people come back physically exhausted but relationally renewed, with a deeper appreciation for one another.

Church-wide picnics and sports events can accomplish the same thing. Trinity sponsors a wonderful picnic every autumn on the polo field near the university. Everyone brings something to eat, and activities are organized for all, making it a cherished celebration.

EVERYONE NEEDS FELLOWSHIP

Shortly after I began seminary, one of my favorite professors provoked us with the thought that "there's more fellowship in a union hall than the average local church." Most of us were shocked by his statement, but it probably held a lot of truth. At the very least, he forced us to think about the importance of relationships in the local church.

Millions of Americans suffer from loneliness. As Craig Ellison has said, it is often the result of negative experiences that leave an individual feeling unaccepted, unattached, and without adequate social skills.[14] The rapid influx of change, the breakdown in the nuclear family, and the mobility of society in general has created a tremendous need for meaningful relationships. The church should be a safe harbor of opportunities for everyone.

This includes pastors. Derek J. Tidball says in *Skillful Shepherds* that pastoral leaders need to remember that shepherds are also sheep, and pastoral support must be mutually given and received. The end result will be that cultural distinctions between "leadership and led" will be reduced.[15] After all, the church is not a business corporation in which roles are narrowly defined and relationships are based on human power and the capricious abuse of authority. Rather, the church is an organism, Christ's body, uniquely designed to reflect the Spirit of the Lord (John 13:34–35).

NOTES

1. Francis Schaeffer, *The Mark of a Christian* (Downers Grove, Ill.: InterVarsity, 1970), 15–26.
2. Win Arn, "Can We Close the Back Door?" *Pastoral Renewal* (February 1986): 117–19.
3. Win Arn, *The Master's Plan for Making Disciples* (Pasadena, Calif.: Church Growth Press, 1982), 77–88.
4. Frank Tillapaugh, *The Church Unleashed* (Ventura, Calif.: Regal, 1982), 134.
5. Keith Huttenlocker, *Becoming the Family of God* (Grand Rapids: Zondervan, 1986), 99.
6. John White, *The Fight* (Downers Grove, Ill.: InterVarsity, 1978), 132.
7. Alan L. McGinnis, *The Friendship Factor* (Minneapolis: Augsburg, 1979), 99.
8. Bruce Larson, "None of Us Are Sinners Emeritus," *Leadership* (Fall 1984): 12–23.
9. Lynn Buzzard, "War and Peace in the Local Church," *Leadership* (Summer 1983): 21–30.
10. Philip Yancey, "The Church As Platypus," *Leadership* (Summer 1986): 104–114.
11. Henry A. Virkler, "The Facilitativeness of Parish Ministers: A Descriptive Study," *Journal of Psychology and Theology* (Summer 1980): 140–46.
12. Larry Richards, *Youth Ministry* (Grand Rapids: Zondervan, 1982), 232.
13. Huttenlocker, *Becoming the Family of God*, 17–24.
14. Craig W. Ellison, "The Roots of Loneliness," *Christianity Today* (10 March 1978): 12–16.
15. Derek J. Tidball, *Skillful Shepherds: An Introduction to Pastoral Theology* (Grand Rapids: Zondervan, 1986), 336.

Chapter 7

Communication: Maintaining Unity and Involvement

Probably more has been written about communication over the past fifty years than about any other topic in organizational behavior.

Andrew D. Szilagyi, Jr.
Organizational Behavior

When Trinity was still a young and relatively small church, communication was no problem. Most church members participated in small groups, which were led by elders of the church. This network gave almost everyone direct personal access to at least one of the church's "key" pastoral leaders.

If someone had a question or concern about the church, all they had to do was ask their small group leader at a regularly scheduled twice-a-month group meeting. Trinity's elders also made a habit of soliciting feedback from their group members regarding church affairs. Their suggestions were frequently implemented, which led to a higher quality of life in the body and a greater sense of "ownership" among church members.

The "sharing" portion of Sunday worship also facilitated communication and helped Trinity maintain a sense of community. This "sharing" time was a ten to fifteen minute period in which people were encouraged to ask questions about the sermon, share prayer requests, and tell others what God had been doing in their lives that week (1 Corinthians 14).

It was also an opportunity for pastoral leaders to inform everyone of upcoming church events or special situations of interest to the entire church. Communication was such that just about everyone knew what was current. The beauty of the system was its simplicity.

Then there was a shift: not sudden, but slow and certain. The lines of communication seemed truncated. And people began complaining.

The complaints had many targets. Some felt that the elders were out of touch with the rest of the body, that they did not know what was going on at the grass roots level, and that they did not seem to care. Others felt that the church was disorganized and certain needs were neglected. For example, some people had to wait six months to join a growth group. Another complaint was expressed concerning the lack of activities for junior high and high school students. One dear lady, a genuinely kindhearted and highly respected member of the church, was so distraught that she wrote the elders a letter, asking, "What's going on here, anyway?"

HOW POOR COMMUNICATION AFFECTED TRINITY

The communication gap, evolving at Trinity over a period of several months, had three major effects. First, the church began to lose the sense of community that had characterized its early days and set it apart from more established (that is, older and larger) churches in the area.

Not everyone felt this to the same degree, but for some it was quite discouraging.

Second, some of the "first generation" members of the church began disengaging themselves from the ministry. Many of them had rendered sacrificial service to establish the church. They were not always highly visible, but they were the type of servants/shepherds that enable a church to realize its potential. For some, their withdrawal was a deliberate choice; for others it was an entirely unconscious response to feeling no longer needed.

Third, the reservoir of generosity and goodwill, previously enabling the church to meet its financial obligations without having to harangue church members for money, began to dry up. Giving slowed down considerably. To put it more bluntly, people began voting with their pocketbooks.

These consequences of broken communication at Trinity exist in other organizations as well. Researchers have long known that activity and involvement are integrally related to a person's knowledge of what is happening.[1] In other words, the more people know about what is going on, the more likely they are to be involved. But while many business corporations are able to thrive in spite of poor internal communication (largely because of their reward systems), most churches cannot because communication in the church is as essential as communication in a marriage. You cannot maintain unity or grow together without it![2]

WHY THE SYSTEM BREAKS DOWN

Communication can break down at the individual, group, or organizational level for a variety of reasons. The main reason Trinity began having problems with communication is that the church tripled in size within fourteen months (going from approximately 150 to 450 members). That type of growth is difficult for any organization to digest, especially if some of the "founders" of the organization move away (as was the case at Trinity).

The elders at Trinity compounded their problems, however, by dropping the "sharing" portion of their worship service without taking the pulse of the congregation first and including them in the decision. The elders just didn't think it would work after they moved into their larger sanctuary. Their decision backfired. A number of people disagreed and believed that they should at least have an opportunity to try to make it work. In addition to the fact that the elders dropped the communication channel (that is, sharing) during worship services, they failed to replace it with anything else, further inflaming the issue.

Rapid growth, however, is not the only reason communication breaks down in a church. Sometimes pastoral leaders (especially staff people and board members) do not understand how much information they have about the inner workings of the church. They are so close to the action that they fail to realize that what is familiar to them is "newsworthy" and of vital interest to other members of the body.

Constant turnover can also create communication problems. The church I now attend has people coming from all over Dallas. Many are young singles, who tend to change churches more frequently than married people. At any rate, several years ago we conducted a church survey which revealed that more than 70 percent of the people in our church had been there less than two years. Membership has stabilized since then, but we're still afflicted .with the transience that typifies metropolitan areas and the "church-hopping" one finds in a city blessed with an abundance of good churches.

Unfortunately, communication also deteriorates rapidly in churches that unknowingly adopt the "exception principle" and "need to know" practices of large corporations.[3] The exception principle works like this: unless the information is something that can be regarded as an "exceptional deviation" from standard operating procedures, do not bother communicating it to management (or, in this case, church members). They are too busy to be bothered with "unimportant items." In reality, many churches would be stronger if church leaders did "bother" to be more open with the congregation about seemingly "unimportant items."

The "need to know" principle works just the opposite. Managers are to be selective and share only the information that people need to know to carry out their tasks effectively. In other words, do not tell the congregation any more than you have to.

Perhaps in highly structured organizations where tasks are relatively simple and routine, it makes sense to operate according to these principles. But in a church community, they're disastrous. After all, the church is a body made up of many members who need each other. It is also a family, and what kind of parent or child would not want to know how or what the rest of their family is doing? As Warren Bennis and Burt Nanus have shown in *Leaders*, their incisive book on leadership, communication is essential to the development of trust, accountability, and reliability.[4]

I am not suggesting that any pastoral leader divulge personal information about another member of the body that has been shared in confidence. For example, there are occasionally individuals or couples who privately come to the elders of our church requesting special prayer for physical or emotional healing. If they want to share their needs with other members of the body (which is often helpful), it's up to them to do so—not the elders. No one has the right to break the trust of another person.

Furthermore, I don't recommend that pastoral leaders begin inundating church members with minutes of every meeting and routine matters. What I'm trying to emphasize is that the larger a church gets, the harder pastoral leaders need to work at keeping people informed of the church's current events—both at the board level and in the rest of the body.

SUGGESTIONS FOR MAINTAINING COMMUNICATION

There's a risk to providing specific suggestions for facilitating communication in the church: it's too tempting to adopt the "programs" without first absorbing and adhering to some "fundamentals." Before implementing any creative ways to communicate, a pastoral leader must (1) understand the importance of communication and (2) develop personal convictions in this area.

If that is accomplished, I'm confident that pastoral leaders will develop communication strategies best suited to the unique characteristics and needs of their church. The following ideas are presented only to stimulate your thinking.

Make the Most of Relationships

As I mentioned in the last chapter, an active, growing church will have numerous overlapping networks of relationships. Pastoral leaders will be ministering "among" the people, visiting them where they work, live, and play, instead of sitting behind big desks in oak-paneled studies waiting for everyone to schedule an appointment.

It is interesting to note that there has been a renaissance in the thinking of more and more corporate leaders on the value of keeping in touch with employees via informal networks. It's frequently referred to as "management by walking around" (MBWA), and it was one of the characteristics of successful companies heralded in the book *In Search of Excellence*.[5] It is amazing what one can learn by lingering around the coffee pot. Just try it before or after one of your church meetings! You'll be surprised at what you can discover!

Use All Your Communication Channels

If you do not already have a monthly church newspaper that covers life in the church, why not start one? The church I attended during college published a monthly newsletter which included a personal letter from one of the elders to explain the issues the elders had been addressing, and request the prayers and input of the congregation on those or any other issues.

The church I now attend has a large kiosk in the main lobby covered with pictures of pastoral leaders and snapshots from current ministries. We also have a booklet explaining the scope of our ministries and listing those to call for help or further information. In addition, we have a "help wanted/ services provided" bulletin board for members of the church.

Other channels of communication that churches can use profitably are as follows: telephone calls, announcements in the bulletin, direct-mail letters (personalized), and special congregational meetings. Eugene Peterson, pastor of Christ Our King Church in Bel Air, Maryland, maintains that practices such as returning telephone calls promptly, answering mail quickly, and publishing a weekly newsletter encourage communication. He also meets spontaneously with small groups of church members to share his concerns about the ministry and to learn what is on their minds.[6]

Don't Worry About Overkill

In general, the larger a church, the more likely it is to suffer from inadequate communication. So don't worry about overdoing it. Most people appreciate any and all efforts made to keep them informed regarding church matters. It is better to bore the members than to ignore them.

SUMMING UP

Over thirty years ago, Robert L. Katz, a professor at Harvard Business School, wrote a classic article in which he discussed the most important skills needed by managers. The thrust of what he said was that good managers need three skills: technical, human, and conceptual.

Technical skills (an understanding of and proficiency in a specific kind of activity) are most important in the early stages of a business career. In other words, if you are an accountant, you better know how to balance the books. If you are a youth pastor, you need to know how to minister to young people.

Conceptual skills, the ability to see the enterprise as a

whole (that is, the big picture), are critical at senior levels. In other words, you need to understand your customers, the competition, and your company. If you are the senior pastor, you need to know how to work with a variety of groups within the church and you need to be sensitive to the needs of the entire congregation.

Human skills (the ability to work with people and maintain effective communication in an organization), however, are important at every stage of a person's business career and largely determine their success.[7] What Dr. Katz discovered over thirty years ago is just as applicable today as it was then—for business managers and church leaders alike.

NOTES

1. Lyle Schaller, *Activating the Passive Church* (Nashville: Abingdon, 1982), 117–18.

2. Larry Richards and Clyde Hoeldtke, *A Theology of Church Leadership* (Grand Rapids: Zondervan, 1980), 337–52.

3. Andrew D. Szilagyi, Jr., and Marc J. Wallace, Jr., *Organizational Behavior and Performance*, 2d ed. (Santa Monica, Calif.: Goodyear, 1980), 426–34.

4. Warren Bennis and Burt Nanus, *Leaders* (New York: Harper & Row, 1985), 21–58.

5. Roger D'Aprix, "The Oldest and Best Way to Communicate With Employees," *Harvard Business Review* (September–October 1982): 30–32.

6. Eugene Peterson, "Haphazardly Intent: An Approach to Pastoring," *Leadership* (Winter 1981): 12–24.

7. Robert L. Katz, "Skills of an Effective Administrator," *Harvard Business Review* (September–October 1974): 90–102.

Chapter 8

Organizational Change: Coping With It Constructively

There is a time for everything, and a season for every activity under heaven.
                                        (Ecclesiastes 3:1)

Our generation demands uncommonly resourceful leaders.
                                        Howard G. Hendricks

Although it is not always obvious, individuals, groups, and organizations are constantly changing. The church is no exception. But when most of us think about change in relation to the pastoral ministry, our focus is usually on individual change—a believer's personal spiritual growth (2 Corinthians 3:18).

What pastoral leaders often overlook and fail to respond to, however, are factors that precipitate change in the church as a whole. I am not thinking here so much of general sociocultural issues (such as secular humanism, the decline in morality, rising divorce rates), but rather of the unique challenges that invariably surface in the life of every church. Consider the following situation at Trinity.

Shortly after Tom joined the staff at Trinity, he presented the elders a plan to develop an adult Sunday school program. Although the church offered classes for adults and children on Wednesday evenings, the turnout was low. People just didn't want to be out another night during the week, and they were voting with their feet. Many, however, had indicated they were interested in educational classes on Sunday mornings. Tom was so excited about the possibilities he could hardly contain his enthusiasm when he shared his ideas with the elders.

Three months and several meetings later, Tom, discouraged and disheartened, withdrew his proposal. He never fully understood why the elders were not in favor of his plan. To this day Trinity still has no adult Sunday school program.

RESISTANCE TO CHANGE

Resistance to change is one of the most baffling problems business managers and pastoral leaders face because it can take so many forms.[1] (See figure 8-4 on page 95.) In Tom's case, the elders' resistance was explicit: they rejected his proposal.

Several years later, when the elders presented church members with a proposal to build a larger sanctuary, they met considerable covert resistance. Few people expressed their opposition directly, but many delayed making pledges.

Researchers have found that the degree to which individuals or organizations resist new programs or methods of operating varies according to the magnitude of the change, the manner in which it is introduced, and the nature of the change itself.[2] In other words, even good ideas may be resisted if (1) they entail a significant change in how things are being done (as was the case with Tom's proposal), or (2) they are poorly introduced (as was the case with the building program).

Fear of the Unknown

Uncertainty about the effects of a proposed change (that is, fear of the unknown) is probably the major obstacle to a church adopting a new idea or way of operating.[3] It certainly derailed Tom's proposal for an adult Sunday school. Even though he presented workable solutions for dealing with problems that might develop as a result of offering the classes (for example, parking, staffing, and overcrowding of children's classes), he could not convince the board that the classes were worth changing the hour of the morning worship service.

Furthermore, he had no guarantee that people would attend the classes. People were concerned that nobody would attend. Worse yet, what if people stopped going to the worship service and only went to an adult Sunday school class? (That was happening in other churches in the area.) At least now patterns were predictable. And as one risk-adverse elder said, "If it isn't broken, don't fix it." The irony in the attitude is that this same individual came to the church as a result of someone taking a risk (rejection) to invite him!

Unwillingness to Give Up Existing Benefits

Ideally, every member of the church should be concerned about the welfare of other members (Philippians 2:3–5). Nevertheless, changes that are good for the body as a whole may, in the short term, have an adverse effect on certain individuals or groups. For example, even though it was difficult for John to admit, he was afraid that attendance at worship services might drop if the church implemented Tom's plan. After all, he would no longer have the benefit of a "captive audience." He would have to "compete" with some of the church's other teachers. And if people did not attend worship services, giving might decrease. He could only envision a downward spiral of reactions.

Many who resisted the construction of a larger sanctuary did so because they did not want to lose the intimacy and sense of community the church had enjoyed. Others did not want to tolerate the inconvenience and headaches that invariably accompany building programs. Some were afraid that Sunday services would become a "production." In short, many people did not want to forego the benefit of feeling comfortable with the status quo. They didn't want to change their ways. To them, the costs of doing things differently (changing) did not outweigh the benefits of keeping things the way they were.

Awareness of Weaknesses in Proposed Changes

Sometimes church members resist change because they are aware of potential problems that have apparently been overlooked. This form of resistance is obviously desirable and had a major impact on Trinity's building program. Initial designs for the new sanctuary were flawed, and cost estimates were overstated. Fortunately, one of the elders contacted a construction engineer for an outside opinion. After examining the plans and cost estimates, he immediately raised objections which led to further study and substantial design changes, thereby saving several hundred thousand dollars. Had the original plan been submitted to the congregation, Trinity's new sanctuary might never have been built. In the end, however, they had a better designed, more energy-efficient, and cost-effective building.

Organizational Structure

Social scientists have long known that individuals and organizations need a certain amount of stability and continuity to function effectively. As Philip Yancey recently wrote, "Organisms with no structure become soft and squishy, and sag in the middle."[4] In the same article, Yancey also points out that the Bible gives little advice on organizational structure. Be that as it may, a church's structure (that is, the way it is organized and operates) can limit its ability to change by restricting the flow of information throughout the church. For example, churches with strong autocratic leaders who emphasize strict adherence to a "chain of command" stifle "negative" feedback that might actually help the church function more effectively.

Resource Limitations

Other churches simply do not have the resources they need to make a particular change. That probably sounds like heresy to some people, but there are times when a church lacks the gifted people or financial resources necessary to accomplish a particular task. For example, a lack of qualified pastoral leaders delayed Trinity's initial plans to establish a sister church. Once they began to consider carefully what would be required, they realized they did not have a large enough core group needed to plant a church. The elders wisely concluded it would be better to wait rather than to push forward understaffed. It is not that they doubted God's ability to provide for their needs; rather, they were being sensitive to the leading of the Holy Spirit.

OVERCOMING RESISTANCE TO CHANGE

Pastoral leaders will seldom be able to entirely overcome everyone's resistance to certain changes. It takes some longer to adjust than others. That does not mean, however, that an idea or proposal should be dropped simply because some people are tied to traditional ways.

For example, Trinity's worship service used to be about two and one-half hours long with a twenty-minute break for refreshments and the introduction of visitors. As visitors were introduced, a member of the church would volunteer to meet them during the break. It made visitors feel at home in the church. When the church was small, the practice worked well.

As Trinity grew and began attracting more visitors, the time set aside for refreshments and introductions expanded to over thirty minutes, thereby disrupting the flow of the worship service. It also made the service unnecessarily long. Sunday school teachers found it difficult to work with children longer than two hours. Moreover, it was impossible to schedule another morning service to relieve overcrowding.

The schedule continued like this for months until a group of parents with small children asked the elders to consider a plan for reducing the length of the service to one and one-half hours. Not only would it make it easier to schedule a second service, it would provide some relief for the teachers in the Sunday school. Visitors would be asked to stand briefly at the end of the service, and would be invited for refreshments afterward. It seemed like an ideal solution.

Not everyone thought so. The younger elders and new staff members liked the idea from the beginning, but the older elders resisted. After hours and hours of discussion, Bob, one of the older elders, candidly admitted that it was hard for him to consider changing the format of the service "because we've always done it this way."

Ironically, Bob had played a major role in founding the church and helping it to develop a more contemporary form of worship. In doing so, he had been challenged by a section of Gene Getz's *Sharpening the Focus of the Church*, which underscores the importance of not allowing nonabsolutes (for example, coffee breaks and the format of worship services) to become absolutes.[5]

The elders eventually decided to streamline the service and eliminate the coffee break in the middle. Bob was not in favor of the change, but he was willing to try it. It took several months for him to feel comfortable with the changes, but eventually even he agreed that they were advantageous.

My point is that different people respond to change differently. Sometimes resistance will come from where it is least expected. Resistance doesn't mean the church lacks unity or single-mindedness. It just means that not everyone thinks alike or readily accepts new ideas. What is important is that people agree on essential things like the nature of the church, its mission, the authority of Scripture, and the ministry of members to one another. Without a sense of oneness on issues like that, it will be impossible to develop real unity and a lasting sense of community.

Recognizing that resistance to change is natural and quite often helpful, pastoral leaders can take the following steps to deal with it constructively. (Please note that denial and retreating to a monastery in southern France are not options!)

Involve Members of the Body in Discussions and Decisions

Plans for Trinity's new sanctuary stalled, until the elders stopped their drive and actively solicited the input of church members. They had assumed that everyone recognized the need for additional space and would be excited about the plan. Communicating with church members *before* they presented the "master plan" would have helped the elders to understand the legitimate needs and concerns of church members, and would have helped to alleviate the fears some people had.

I am not suggesting that every decision pastoral leaders make needs to be submitted to a congregational vote, but if a proposed change is significant enough and/or affects a large portion of the church, it should be processed with church members before it is set in concrete. Many church members are willing to make amazing sacrifices to see their church bear fruit, but they need to sense that pastoral leaders care about their thoughts and feelings. They also want to be able to contribute to the decision-making process.

Support of Respected Pastoral Leaders

A major reason why Trinity was finally able to build a larger sanctuary is that the plan gained the support of a broad spectrum of respected pastoral leaders. As a result, it was not thought of as the pastor's idea, the board's idea, or the building committee's idea. It was the body's idea. As more and more pastoral leaders began to understand and support the project, other members of the congregation followed suit.

Cynics refer to this as the "herd instinct"; positive thinkers call it "leadership by example."

Conversely, one of the reasons Tom's proposal for an adult Sunday school program never materialized is that it never had the support of any highly regarded pastoral leaders. Had Tom waited a little longer and given people time to get to know him better, his idea might have been accepted.

Provide Regular Progress Reports

Once Trinity's pastoral leaders confirmed that it was God's will for them to go forward with the building program, they kept church members well-informed of all developments (for example, building plans, zoning meetings, donations, etc.). They were committed to being "low-key" with respect to financial needs, but when the church received a significant donation from outside the body, they used it as a cause for celebration.

In the same way, they provided regular feedback on the results of streamlining worship services. Teachers were happier, parents were relieved, and parking problems were solved. In short, many of the causes of resistance were resolved, and encouraging things were happening. Conveying this to church members helped everyone adjust to the changes more quickly.[6]

RECOGNIZING WHEN CHANGES ARE NEEDED

Pastoral leaders are called to deal with many relatively minor changes, requiring simple adjustments in procedures. Other changes, such as building a new sanctuary, are so large that the need for careful planning is obvious. There are occasions, however, when even the most conscientious pastoral leader may fail to recognize the need for change. What follows, is a brief discussion of some symptoms that could indicate that a change is necessary.

First of all, when key people disengage from the ministry or leave the church, it may be a sign that something is amiss—that a change needs to be made. When the elders matter-of-factly doubled the size of Trinity's small groups, several key group leaders dropped out shortly thereafter. In addition to the fact that the elders had been heavy-handed, the large groups were functioning poorly. A change was needed. In this case, it was a change back to the old way of doing things.

Second, when people start complaining, a change may need to be made. For example, when the congregation started complaining about the elders being isolated and out of touch with the body, it was clear that the elders needed to do a better job of communicating and soliciting input from the church members.

When several people voiced their concerns about the elders increasing the size of the small groups, the elders ignored it. Unable to generate any change, many dropped out. Of course, there is a right and a wrong way to "complain," but regardless of the spirit with which concerns are expressed, pastoral leaders have an obligation to listen carefully.

Third, when a church's growth plateaus, while other churches in the area continue to grow, it may be a sign that changes are needed. Perhaps members of the body have lost their sense of mission and are no longer reaching out to others in the community.

DEALING CONSTRUCTIVELY WITH CHANGE

Dealing constructively with change does not mean that pastoral leaders should dilute doctrinal convictions. Nor does it mean that they should encourage people to conform to the culture in which they live (Romans 12:2). There are biblical absolutes, and there is such a thing as right and wrong! Not everything, however, is a watershed issue that merits being defended to the last breath. Furthermore, there are many creative ways to minister. As Dr. Hendricks said, "Our generation needs uncommonly resourceful leaders." It does not need wishy-washy, unprincipled, country-club Christians (James 1:5–8; 2 Timothy 2:1–7).

Nor does dealing constructively with change require trying to please everyone. One of the most sobering lessons I learned as a young elder is that it is impossible to please everyone. God requires that pastoral leaders be faithful, sensitive to the leading of the Holy Spirit, and servant-shepherds—not obsequious people-pleasers (1 Thessalonians 2:3–6).

Finally, dealing constructively with change does not mean that pastoral leaders should experiment loosely with trendy ministry techniques. I briefly attended a church during the late seventies that began several encounter groups. Although I believe group counseling can meet multiple needs of the local church, it requires highly trained group leaders and skillful supervision. Simply encouraging people to "get in touch with their feelings," without helping them understand those feelings can result in chaos or real damage to the people.

On the other hand, dealing constructively with change *does* require pastoral leaders to be aware of what is going on around them. They must face reality. As Keith Huttenlocker states in his captivating book *Becoming the Family of God*, many people bring excess baggage to the church. Some expect pastoral leaders to be the perfect parent they never had. Others think that the Lord's body should be free from conflict (as if sin did not exist). The truth is that no church is perfect. Furthermore, any growing church is bound to have growing pains.

Handling change constructively also requires that pastoral leaders understand and deal effectively with resistance—and that they help other members of the body do the same. When changes need to be made, they need to be made with sensitivity to the needs of the entire community, not just the demands of a vocal few.

Whenever I think about the changes churches have to deal with, the Jerusalem Council comes to mind (Acts 15). Imagine the situation Peter, Paul, James, and Barnabus were facing. The rapid progress of Gentile evangelization in Antioch was bringing forth an era in which there would be more Gentile Christians than Jewish Christians. The Jewish Christians were afraid that the rapid influx of Gentiles into the church would result in a decline in moral standards (that is, negative changes). Was not the Corinthian church proof of this?

How were the Jewish Christians going to handle the situation? They knew they had to admit believing Gentiles into the church, but to maintain some form of quality control, they insisted that the Gentiles be circumcised and keep the Mosaic Law. Talk about resistance to change! Had those proscriptions been enforced they might have had a ripple effect throughout the Christian world—and the church might never have flourished the way it did.[7]

LOOKING FORWARD

In January 1986, *Christianity Today* published a comprehensive report written by fellows and resource scholars of the Christianity Today Institute. The report, "Into the Next Century: Trends Facing the Church," addressed the challenges and trends most likely to influence the church for the rest of the twentieth century (fig. 8-1).[8]

Figure 8-1
**Trends and Challenges Facing the Church
in the United States**

1. *More "religion," less impact*
   Evangelicals have greater visibility (as in publishing, education, and politics), but is it making any difference in society?

2. *Rising expectations among the world's poor*
   Approximately 20 million people go hungry in America. How will the church respond?

3. *The graying of America*
   Most church programs are geared toward youth. As the population ages, the church will need to develop new approaches to ministry.

4. *The coloring of America*
   The American church is changing along racial and ethnic lines. Maintaining unity amid diversity will be difficult.

5. *The end of female passivity*

Roles for women in society are changing. Only 21 percent are "full-time homemakers." More and more women are attending seminary. Many are looking for greater leadership roles in the local church.

6. *Secular humanism within the church*
   Although the quality of Americans professing Christian belief is encouraging, Evangelicals have not recognized the degree to which secular humanism has invaded the church.

7. *Growing "me-ism" and materialism*
   The bonfires of selfishness are being fueled by the gasoline of affluence.

8. *Shifting denominational power*
   Population shifts and a decline in membership will force mainline denominations to decentralize and become more democratic.

9. *Pluralism gone to seed*
   The church is polarized on many issues, which makes it more difficult for non-Christians to understand and embrace Christianity.

10. *A tilt toward the relational*
    The longing for human intimacy and a search for spiritual experience reflect the impact of technology and secularism on society.

Source: Christianity Today Institute, "Into the Next Century: Trends Facing the Church," *Christianity Today* (17 January 1986): 2–31.

As I thought about the issues raised in the report, I couldn't help but reflect on the changes I had encountered as an elder in the local church—and how thoroughly unprepared I was to respond to those changes (let alone anticipate them). But I have also learned that the body of Christ is an incredibly resilient organism, quite able to survive and even thrive in the midst of great turmoil. As Christ said, "I will build My church; and the gates of Hades shall not overpower it" (Matthew 16:18 NASB).

In all likelihood, the church will continue to confront major changes in years ahead. Pastoral leaders do not, however, need to fear change. As the psalmist said, "God is . . . an ever-present help" (Psalm 46:1). Furthermore, the basic needs of mankind and the mission of the church have not changed in more than two thousand years and are unlikely to do so in the next two hundred.

Managing the ministry will, however, become increasingly challenging. It will require pastoral leaders who are flexible and responsive to change.[9] Furthermore, as the average size of churches increases (due to the ongoing urbanization of the population), pastoral leaders will need to be able to deal with what Daniel J. Isenberg refers to as "portfolios of problems": issues and opportunities which (1) exist simultaneously, (2) compete for attention, and (3) are interrelated.[10]

There is one certainty here. Churches that lose sight of their mission and fail to deal with change constructively will stop growing. Stunted growth will eventually bring death. (See figures 8-2, 8-3, and 8-4.)

Figure 8-2
Organizational Change

Sources of Resistance	Overcoming Resistance
1. Fear of the unknown	1. Involve members of the body in discussions and decisions
2. Unwillingness to forfeit existing benefits	2. Support of respected pastoral leaders
3. Awareness of weaknesses in proposed changes	3. Provide regular progress reports
4. Organization structure	4. Prayer and fasting
5. Resource limitations	

Figure 8-3
Variations in Organizational Change
A Systems Overview

Explanation: A systems approach to management views an organization as a unified, purposeful system composed of interrelated parts (that is, an organism vs. an institution). It also emphasizes the importance of looking at an organization as a whole because a change in one of the variables shown above usually results in a change in one or more of the others.

Application to the Church: Changing the nature of a *task* can affect relationships among individuals and groups in the church. Every church has an explicit or implicit *structure* that shapes the working relationships of its members. The *people* variable applies to members of the church (including their attitudes, personalities, and motivations). *Technology* encompasses such items as computers, typewriters, VCRs, tape recorders, radio, and television.

Figure 8-4
A Sample of Major Changes at Trinity

	Areas Affected			
Nature of the Change	People	Task	Structure	Technology
Location changes (3)	X	X	X	X
Tom's resignation	X	X	X	
Rapid growth	X	X	X	X
Increased size of groups	X	X	X	
Altered format of services	X	X	X	
Erected new building	X	X	X	X
Key elders left	X	X	X	

NOTES

1. James A. F. Stoner, *Management* (Englewood Cliffs, N.J.: Prentice-Hall, 1978), 372–95.

2. Andrew D. Szilagyi, Jr., and Marc J. Wallace, Jr., *Organizational Behavior and Performance,* 2d ed. (Santa Monica, Calif.: Goodyear, 1980), 522–50.

3. Don Hellriegel, John W. Slocum, and Richard W. Woodman, *Organizational Behavior,* 4th ed. (New York: West, 1986), 573–80.

4. Philip Yancey, "The Church As Platypus," *Leadership* (Summer 1986): 104–113.

5. Gene Getz, *Sharpening the Focus of the Church* (Chicago: Moody, 1974), 155–75.

6. Thomas J. Peters and Robert H. Waterman, Jr., *In Search of Excellence* (New York: Harper & Row, 1982), 99.

7. F. F. Bruce, *Commentary on the Book of Acts* (Grand Rapids: Eerdmans, 1979), 298–320.

8. Christianity Today Institute, "Into the Next Century: Trends Facing the Church," *Christianity Today* (17 January 1986): 2–31.

9. Craig Hickman and Michael Silva, *Creating Excellence* (New York: New American Library, 1984), 77–95.

10. Daniel J. Isenberg, "How Senior Managers Think," *Harvard Business Review* (November–December 1984): 81–90.

Chapter 9

Small Groups: Facilitating Fellowship and Ministry

Every healthy local church will have not only the united service of dignity on the Lord's day, but it will divide the congregation into fellowship groups, which meet in each other's home during the week. We need both; we must not choose between them.[1]

John R. W. Stott

After several years of relative peace and quiet, the number of small groups operating at Trinity quadrupled. The necessary organizational change for this was astounding. To borrow Charles Dickens's opening line in *A Tale of Two Cities*, it was the best of times and the worst of times.

When the dust finally settled, over half the congregation was participating in a variety of small groups: growth groups, Bible studies, prayer groups. It was exciting. Members of the body were getting to know others in the church, using their spiritual gifts, and growing.

However, as mentioned earlier, problems did develop. Specifically, Trinity ran out of qualified group leaders. Others burned themselves out. Waiting lists developed. Some groups became what C. John Miller, pastor of New Life Presbyterian Church in Philadelphia, Pennsylvania, refers to as "protective spiritual nests for garden-variety people." In other words, instead of being a base of edification and ministry outreach, the small group became a stagnant and ingrown comfort center.[2] Some people began changing groups frequently, creating confusion. All this only confirms that small groups can be a "challenge" to manage. And the elders at Trinity were not prepared to deal with some of the unfolding basic problems. Focusing on the following factors would have helped Trinity's pastoral leaders to reduce confusion, eliminate unnecessary turnover, and maintain a smooth course.

EXPLAINING THE PURPOSE OF A GROUP

The most critical omission of the pastoral leaders at Trinity was their failure to explain the purpose of a group to people *before* people joined.[3] (See figure 9-1.) This is imperative since all groups are not the same. Growth groups, for example, had always been the primary small group at Trinity. They were made up of ten to fifteen members who met together semimonthly for Bible study, prayer, and fellowship. (Elsewhere similar groups may be called "mini-churches," "action groups," or "koinonia groups.")

At any rate, as the number of growth groups began multiplying, Trinity's elders discovered that the term "growth group" meant different things to different people. Some thought it was a Bible study; others believed it was mainly a social time; a few thought it was group counseling.

Confusion stemmed partially from the fact that several groups operated differently. Furthermore, several people at Trinity had previous experience in small groups that shaped their expectations. For example, individuals who had been in a small-group setting with Inter-Varsity Christian Fellowship during college tended to think growth groups would provide

Figure 9-1
Types of Groups

	Mini-Church	Bible Study	Discipleship Group	Mothers Encouragement Group	Prayer Group	Shepherding Group	Dinner for Eight
PURPOSE	Ministry Fellowship Maturity	Fellowship Education	Discipling Skills development	Fellowship Support Encouragement	Prayer	Fellowship Encouragement	Socializing Networking
COMMITMENT	Very high	High	Very high	Moderate	Moderate	High	Moderate
FREQUENCY OF MEETINGS	Semimonthly	Weekly	Weekly	Weekly	Weekly	Quarterly	Weekly
DURATION	Ongoing	6–12 weeks	6–9 months	Ongoing	Ongoing	12 months	4–6 weeks
SIZE	15–20	5–15	8–12	10–30	3+	8–10	8
OPEN/CLOSED*	Closed	Both	Closed	Open	Open	Open	Closed

*Open groups admit new members at any time. Closed groups usually admit new members only when someone drops out or a new group is formed.

the same experiences. Sometimes that happened; sometimes it didn't.

Whatever the type of group, to minimize confusion and help people participate meaningfully, it is essential to communicate its purpose clearly. It helps to do this verbally and in writing via brochures and announcements.[4]

In addition to reducing unnecessary turnover, a clear statement of purpose saves time and energy otherwise wasted when people join a group and quickly drop out because it is not designed to meet their needs. As one of Trinity's growth group leaders said, "Nothing is more discouraging than to have someone join a growth group when what they really wanted was an intensive Bible study." David A. Womack, pastor of Twin Palms Assembly of God in San Jose, California, has lucidly stated, "People do not come to homes primarily for Bible study. Rather, they are attracted by their needs for social interaction, the support of caring and sharing friends, and a sense of belonging to a meaningful body of peers."[5]

Long-term groups should review their purpose every six months and encourage members to reevaluate their role in the group. This helps group members to maintain a high level of commitment, enables the group(s) to stay on target, and makes it possible for group members to bow out gracefully as the Spirit leads.

RECRUITING AND TRAINING GROUP LEADERS

Perhaps the biggest problem Trinity encountered with small groups is that the need for willing *and* able group leaders exceeded the supply. For a long time Trinity relied heavily on members of the congregation who had prior experience leading small groups in parachurch ministries like Inter-Varsity, Campus Crusade for Christ, and the Navigators.

After exhausting those resources (literally and figuratively), the elders turned to people who had experience participating in existing groups and had shown some "leadership ability." Although they discovered several good leaders, the elders unintentionally coerced some saints into shepherding positions for which they were not gifted. As a result, both the shepherds and the sheep suffered. The shepherds felt discouraged for having tried something and failed. The sheep felt confused and disappointed. The latter were encouraged to join other groups. The former were handled with tenderness and care, and encouraged to use their gifts in other areas of ministry.

It took almost five years for the elders at Trinity to come to grips with the fact that they needed to provide ongoing training for group leaders. Once they did, they quickly learned why so many churches struggle with how to go about it—it's hard work and practical models are scarce. After months of research, several visits to other churches, and a lot of trial and error, Trinity's pastoral leaders developed an effective approach to training group leaders.

Discipleship Groups

Although Trinity occasionally had special training seminars, discipleship groups were the church's primary means for training group leaders. The purpose of the groups was to equip people to (1) study the Bible, (2) develop their relationship with God, and (3) minister in small groups.

The objectives for the training on ministering in small groups were to teach how to (1) lead an inductive Bible study, (2) facilitate sharing, and (3) lead a group in prayer. One of the key assumptions underlying the training was that people learn best by doing, especially when learning skills related to leading groups.

Groups were limited to ten to twelve people so that everyone had an opportunity to participate. They were composed of couples and singles, and most met once a week for ten weeks. At every meeting, a different member of the group was responsible for leading one part of the meeting (such as Bible study, prayer, or sharing). All were expected to participate.

Group members were also provided (at no cost) with

101

materials: (1) a notebook filled with information about small groups, inductive Bible studies, and (2) some basic reading materials like *Growth Groups* and Em Griffin's *Getting Together*, a Navigators booklet titled *Leading Bible Study Discussions*, and an Inter-Varsity book called *Leading Inductive Bible Studies*. These materials contain a wealth of information on group dynamics.

The genius of the training process Trinity developed was that (1) it focused on developing three skills essential to leading a variety of small groups, (2) it was well organized, (3) it was practical and easy to adapt to almost any church, and (4) it was relatively brief.

Furthermore, one reason why the training was so effective is that everyone who participated did so voluntarily (because they were highly motivated). Not everyone who completed the training became a group leader, but those who wanted to do so had the basic skills required to do a good job.

Trinity offered training like this at least twice a year for anyone who desired it (or as often as needed). It took Trinity's pastoral leaders much time and hard work to develop their program, and it is continually being improved, but the elders have been convinced it has been essential to the church's long-term growth and development. In fact, many of the people who have finished the training consider it "life-changing," and many volunteered to take a leadership role in one of the church's small-group ministries.

PROVIDING SUPPORT AND MAINTAINING OVERSIGHT

When the number of groups operating at Trinity began expanding rapidly, Trinity's elders knew they needed to develop a means for maintaining oversight. They did not want to dominate the groups, but they needed to stay abreast of what was going on. Furthermore, they wanted the input of group leaders. After all, they were the primary pastoral caregivers in the church.

Shepherding Groups

To facilitate communication between elders and growth group leaders, Trinity formed several shepherding groups comprised of an elder and four to five couples leading growth groups. These groups met for potluck dinners every two to three months to discuss the ministry, encourage one another, and pray for the church. Leading or participating in a shepherding group was optional because the elders did not want to burden people with too many meetings. A designated staff person (Tom) or another elder kept in touch with those not in a shepherding group.

Trinity learned the hard way that a shepherding-group leader should either be leading a growth group or be a highly respected pastoral leader with previous small-group experience. At one time, Trinity had a shepherding-group leader who knew little about groups and had never been involved in a growth group. Although he was an elder and meant well, he was not able to minister effectively to the group leaders.

Trinity has found that it helps to change the composition of shepherding groups every six to twelve months. This enables group leaders to meet others in the church and to learn more about how other groups operate.

Designated Staff

Besides forming shepherding groups, the elders at Trinity designated a staff person (Tom) to be responsible for overseeing the church's small-group ministries. This responsibility encompassed growth groups, Bible studies, discipleship groups, and a support group for young mothers called Mom-to-Mom. The staff person's responsibilities included determining what needs exist, recruiting and training group leaders, placing people in groups, and informing the elders.

Tom was assigned the responsibility because he was highly respected. He also had good pastoral and organizational skills, the patience of Job, and knowledge of and experience with a variety of small groups. He was not "in charge" of all the groups (or their leaders); rather, he was a servant to and resource person for the leaders and other staff members who worked with small groups.

Steering Committee

Once every four to six weeks, Tom met over breakfast with a handful of other small-group leaders. Most were also shepherding-group leaders. During their time together, they discussed how the groups are doing, reviewed which groups were interested in adding new members (placement), discussed needs for training, processed special problems, and prayed for the ministry. Being a member of the steering committee was strictly voluntary and required only a six-to-twelve-month commitment. In addition to helping Tom keep in touch with the needs of the groups, it allowed other pastoral leaders to contribute significantly to the direction of the ministry.

Establishing Guidelines for Meetings

When a couple of growth groups started serving wine at their meetings (causing some church members to stumble), Trinity's elders realized that it is occasionally necessary for the elders to establish guidelines regarding group meetings. Because it was potentially divisive, the elders met with several group leaders and concluded that for the sake of church unity it would be best to discontinue the practice of serving wine. The issue was openly discussed and all growth group leaders agreed. Controversial situations like this, however, rarely occurred and Trinity's groups enjoyed a great deal of autonomy in how they functioned.

Providing Resources

Another area in which a church can support small-group ministries is providing group leaders with ministry resources. For example, any group leader at Trinity could use the church's copying machine to reproduce handouts for group meetings. In addition, group leaders were given books and articles related to their ministry. It may seem like a small gesture, but it showed group leaders that they were appreciated, which means a lot to those who minister without receiving much recognition.

PREPARING PEOPLE TO PARTICIPATE

In the early days of Trinity's small-group ministry, people filled out a sign-up sheet, turned it into the church office, and were more or less arbitrarily placed in groups. The problem with this procedure was that Trinity's pastoral leaders were assuming that people (1) knew what they were signing up for, and (2) did not care what group they joined. Both assumptions were wrong. Most individuals want to have a say about the group they join. For that matter, they should, because it often requires a big commitment. Although it initially means more work for the church staff and group leaders, in the long run it is worth the effort to give people as much information as possible about the nature of a particular group(s) so that they can understand their alternatives and choose wisely. People should also be encouraged to network and join friends in existing groups.

Commitment

Another lesson many group leaders learn the hard way is that if you do not stress the importance of commitment, you will always have problems with attendance, which will prevent the group(s) from becoming cohesive. Nothing kills cohesiveness more quickly than one or two group members staying home because they were "tired" or "didn't have time to complete their Bible study." The commitment required to participate in a particular group should vary according to the type of group.

As a general rule, Trinity's growth group members were expected to attend meetings unless they were ill (or had an illness in their family), had out-of-town relatives or friends visiting them, were on vacation, or had unavoidable work conflicts. Unexplained absenteeism is usually a sign that something is wrong.

I began to understand the message behind poor attendance a few years ago when one of the couples in our group began missing meetings. Once I finally acknowledged that a problem existed, I met them for lunch to find out how they felt about the group. As it turned out, they felt threatened by the intimacy level of the group and chose to drop out.

The commitment level for some Bible studies may also be high. For example, in the church I now attend, if people do not think they can attend 75 percent of regularly scheduled meetings, they are encouraged to find another group better suited to their schedule or to postpone joining until they can attend more meetings. One reason why we feel comfortable doing this is that we have Bible study meetings scheduled at different hours almost every day of the week. Had Trinity adopted a similar approach when it first began its small groups, it could have avoided needless turnover.

Logistics

Regardless of the type of group, people need to know how often the group will meet, where it will meet, and for how long. Individual groups can make adjustments as their needs dictate, but the basic patterns should be established before the group begins. Otherwise, it becomes confusing for everyone.

Confidentiality

The importance of confidentiality should be stressed continually for the simple reason that people are more willing to join and remain in a small group if they know that matters shared in group meetings will not be divulged to others outside the group. The group I am in now rarely has problems with this, largely because we stress its importance.

Realistic Expectations

Encourage prospective members to develop realistic expectations. There is no such thing as a perfect group. Leaders make mistakes, and members are fallible. Furthermore, it takes time for any group to gel. One of the best discipleship groups in our church started out very slowly. I will never forget when one of its members called me up to share his discouragement. His group was filled with wonderful people and had an experienced group leader. But the interactions just were not coming together like (or when) he thought they would. I encouraged him to be patient and give it a little more time. Two weeks later he was so excited about his group he could not stop talking about it.

Figure 9-2
Advantages of a Small Group

1. It is flexible.
2. It is mobile.
3. It is inclusive.
4. It is personal.
5. It can grow by division.
6. It can be an effective means of evangelism.
7. It requires a minimum of professional leadership.
8. It is adaptable to the institutional church.

Source: Howard Snyder, *The Problem of Wineskins* (Downers Grove, Ill.: InterVarsity, 1977).

THE MINISTRY OF SMALL GROUPS

In his superb book, *A Challenge to Care*, Charles Simpson correctly states that small groups are a key to a church being able to grow large in size while preserving personal care and a sense of belonging (that is, community).[6] As mentioned earlier, the groups play a major role in the church accomplishing its mission. But managing small groups, whether it is five or twenty-five, can try the patience of the noblest of saints. Being clear about the purpose of a group, preparing people to participate, providing support, and continually grooming new leaders will help to maximize the blessings for everyone.

And the blessings are substantial. Researchers continue to show that one of the biggest needs in the country today, among both Christians and non-Christians, is for personal relationships.[7] The church is in an excellent position to capitalize on this trend by providing a well-managed network of small groups (figs. 9-2 and 9-3).

Figure 9-3
Managing Small Groups

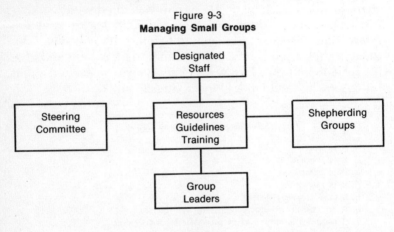

NOTES

1. John R. W. Stott, "Setting the Spirit Free," *Christianity Today* (12 June 1981): 56.

2. C. John Miller, *Outgrowing the Ingrown Church* (Grand Rapids: Zondervan, 1986), 161–74.

3. Kevin Springer, "The Theory and Practice of Small Groups," *Pastoral Renewal* (September 1986): 1, 13–16.

4. Em Griffin, *Getting Together: A Guide for Good Groups* (Downers Grove, Ill.: InterVarsity, 1982), 15–46.

5. David A. Womack, "Five Small-Group Myths," *Leadership* (Winter 1986): 118–22.

6. Charles Simpson, *The Challenge to Care* (Ann Arbor, Mich.: Servant, 1986), 119–30.

7. George Barna, "SGL Conversation With George Barna," *The Small Group Letter* 4:4 (July–August 1987): 3–4.

PART III

Chapter 10

Strategic Planning:
An Effective Approach

The plans of the diligent lead to profit as surely as haste leads to poverty. (Proverbs 21:5)

Proper planning recognizes that God's sovereign will is the final determiner of the outcome.

Garry Friesen
Decision Making and the Will of God

Shortly after I was ordained and began serving as an elder, the senior pastor "volunteered" me to coordinate the church's strategic planning process. Actually, the church did not have a strategic planning process; he wanted me to institute one. Why? Basically because the church was growing and he thought the elders needed to be thinking long-term. I was anointed because the pastor thought my seminary training, church involvement, business education, and work experience had prepared me for such a task.

111

Although I wanted to be helpful, I pleaded incompetence (like Moses) and immediately nominated someone else for the "opportunity." After all, I was the youngest and newest member of the board. The pastor's confidence in me notwithstanding, I did not feel qualified either. As it turned out, no one else wanted to do it, which puzzled me. How could anyone turn down such a golden opportunity? Didn't they know that MBA students drool over the chance to do strategic planning? Apparently not.

To make a long story short, I humbly accepted the job, took a deep breath, and started work. Soon thereafter, I began to understand why no one else was interested in the job.

ROADBLOCKS TO PLANNING

"It Isn't Spiritual"

One of the first stumbling blocks I had to overcome is that a lot of people think it is not spiritual to plan anything— and especially not church matters. Although they seldom say so directly, they think it shows a lack of faith. After all, if God sovereignly controls everything that happens, what point is there in making any plans?

Frankly, this mentality was difficult for me to cope with, so I sought the counsel of a respected Christian businessman who was active as a director of several Christian organizations. Much to my dismay, I discovered that he did not put much stock in planning either. In fact, whenever the subject of strategic planning came up at his company, he would quote Proverbs 3:5–6, "Trust in the LORD with all your heart, and lean not on your own understanding." Then he would dismiss the subject.

Believing firmly in the doctrine of common sense, which says that planning can be beneficial, I began searching the Scriptures for some support and reread parts of Garry Friesen's *Decision Making and the Will of God.*

Two of the most helpful passages I came across were Proverbs 21:5 and James 4:13–16. In addition to stating that the plans of the diligent lead to advantage, Proverbs 21:5 suggests that failing to plan may lead to hasty actions—and poverty.

In James 4:13–16, James clearly criticizes the arrogant presumption of business people who develop short-range ("today or tomorrow") and long-range ("spend a year") plans without considering God. But as Friesen points out, James never reproves the practice of planning itself. What he criticizes is a lack of humility and failure to recognize God's sovereignty in the process. That *is* unbiblical.[1]

Finally, I was encouraged by Scriptures that show that the apostle Paul made both short-range (Acts 20:16; 1 Corinthians 4:19) and long-range plans (Acts 18:21; 19:21; 1 Corinthians 16:5–7). In fact, many of Paul's travel plans came to pass (Acts 18:21; 1 Timothy 3:14). For example, after numerous delays, he finally made it to Spain (Romans 15:25–28).

Does that mean that Paul was not trusting God, that he was trying to force or manipulate events so they would turn out his way? Not at all! What it does demonstrate is that Paul was sensitive to the leading of the Holy Spirit and submitted himself to the sovereignty of God. He knew from experience that "In his heart a man plans his course, but the LORD determines his steps" (Proverbs 16:9).

Furthermore, as Peter Wagner points out in *Strategies for Church Growth*, God himself has a plan for the world, a plan that demanded sacrificing his own Son (John 3:16). Human and divine aspects of spreading the gospel, both of which require planning, are beautifully captured in 1 Corinthians 3:6–7, which says that Paul planted, Apollos watered, but God gave the increase![2]

"It Doesn't Make Any Difference"

Another major criticism of strategic planning is that it does not make any difference. Unfortunately, this complaint is usually well-founded. Simply stated, planning becomes a waste of time because (1) goals and objectives are usually so vague that they are difficult to implement, and (2) no one is clearly assigned responsibility for implementation. Hence, results are negligible at best. That's one of the reasons Proverbs 21:5 is so important. It directly links planning with diligence. The planning of the "diligent" leads to advantage because diligent people follow through. The process itself may be intellectually stimulating and expand one's awareness. The plans of individuals (or groups) who do not follow through, however, are worthless.

The failure to see tangible results from planning was an issue that really bothered one of my fellow elders. He had been on the boards of several churches and had seen many strategic plans come and go without making much difference. His lack of enthusiasm for my "high calling" was understandable. For that matter, a number of business executives have become increasingly disenchanted with strategic planning for similar reasons. As a result, many companies are scaling back their corporate planning staffs. Others are taking steps to develop more detailed action plans and improve implementation.[3]

"It Takes Too Much Time"

Planning frustrates many people because they think it too time consuming (and, by implication, not worth the effort). I have to admit that planning can be painful, and it definitely takes time. But it is not a fruitless task. Neither is it an impossible one. The reason it often seems impossible is that people with good intentions try to accomplish too much and become consumed by a quagmire of details. The tendency to gather more information than necessary is especially prevalent in the business world because it is a socially acceptable way to avoid making decisions. More and more researchers are showing that sound planning and successful operations (profitability) do not require extensive analyses of competitors and the external environment. Rather, the focus should be on superior execution.[4] Implementation and administration are topics that will be addressed more fully in the next chapter.

Strategic planning is not a panacea for every disease that ails the church, and it is tempting to blame the planning process instead of inefficient follow-up. As we shall see later, it can actually save time and help pastoral leaders avoid a host of unnecessary problems.

The Survival Instinct at Work

Perhaps the most pervasive reason why churches and other nonprofit organizations fail to plan is that they are too busy maintaining day-to-day operations. Long-term planning is a luxury they think they cannot afford. This is especially true in smaller organizations forced to operate with very lean and almost all volunteer staffs. Every day brings a sufficient number of "challenges and opportunities." There seems to be no point to worrying about tomorrow (Matthew 6:34).

I am firmly committed to enjoying life and living in the "here and now," and I know how excruciating it is to have more to do than is humanly possible. But I also know the benefits of planning are priceless and worth every moment of prerequisite working time.

THE BENEFITS OF PLANNING

Ministry Focus

One of my seminary professors used to say, "If you don't know where you're going, any road will take you there." Churches that neglect planning frequently find themselves with diffuse programs that have little to do with the Great Commission. One of the greatest benefits of strategic planning is that it provides consistent guidance for the church by helping pastoral leaders to focus on the basic mission of the church: worship, edification, and evangelism.

For example, one reason why the elders at Trinity decided not to devote church resources to a political action movement for voter registration was that their prior planning showed that this activity—however valuable—did not fall within the parameters of what God had called them to do. It also reflected an approach to ministry similar to that of Robert Schuller, pastor of Garden Grove Community Church in California. Whenever the church board considers a new ministry, they ask three questions: (1) Would it be a great thing for God? (2) Would it help people who are hurting? and (3) Is anybody else doing the job? With respect to the last of the three, unless someone is doing the job in an ineffective or clumsy way, Schuller recommends cooperating with them. That is the essence of "possibility-thinking."[5]

Sensitivity to Needs

Another benefit of planning is that it encourages pastoral leaders to remain sensitive to the leading of the Holy Spirit and the current needs of the people to whom God has called them to minister. Certain basic needs, of course, never change. For example, all Christians need to understand their spiritual gifts and know how they fit in the body of Christ. But society is constantly changing and forcing God's people to deal with new sets of problems. When I was in high school, teenage pregnancies were rare and abortion was unheard of. Today Christian young people are continually bombarded with explicit messages that condone premarital sex and abortion. How should a church respond? Certainly not by pretending the world has not changed or that the problems do not exist!

Unfortunately, a number of church leaders have buried their heads in their pillows and have continued to replicate the same programs year after year without ever taking time to think creatively about the changing needs of their congregation or community. And yet one of the major characteristics of successful companies heralded in *In Search of Excellence* is their intense efforts to "stay close to the customer" to serve their needs effectively. For example, IBM's senior managers continually evaluate the customers' needs and try to respond to every complaint within twenty-four hours.[6]

Anticipating Change

Planning can also help pastoral leaders anticipate and deal more constructively with change. As mentioned in chapter 8 when Trinity was a young church and had only a few small groups, managing them was no problem. But when the church started growing, it naturally became more difficult to operate the groups. Failure to plan on how to deal with the church's growth and the need for leadership training created chaos.

In contrast, Tom, responsible for Christian education, regularly made long-range plans for the children's ministry and was able to anticipate the need for additional Sunday school teachers. He was also able to cope more constructively with the space constraints that developed as a result of the church's rapid growth.

No one can fully predict future events, but certain probable changes can be expected. Planning can help pastoral leaders deal more effectively with some of the obvious changes. The ability to anticipate and respond with versatility to change is such an important issue in corporate America that the authors of *Creating Excellence* listed it as one of the six major skills most needed by business executives to lead their organizations effectively. The church needs leaders with this skill. By saying this I am not implying that God doesn't effect his will in the midst of inflexible, short-sighted leaders. He does. But the beauty of the church is its resilience, ability to impart contemporary culture, and faithfulness to God.[7] This attractiveness can be enhanced by capable, visionary leadership.

Coordination and Unity

Planning can also generate greater church unity as a result of better coordinated church activities. When churches are young and fairly small, coordinating church programs is seldom problematic. But as churches grow and the number of its programs multiplies, it becomes increasingly important to plan certain aspects carefully.

For example, our church offers educational classes and ministry training on Wednesday nights for everyone in the church. At one point, a major discipleship group ministry in our church considered having meetings on the same night. Not everyone, of course, was interested in being involved in both, but the elders were afraid that scheduling both at the same time would significantly limit attendance. The solution was fairly simple. The leaders of the discipleship group ministry agreed to schedule their meetings on another night of the week, thereby avoiding a conflict and enabling people to participate in both. In this case, strategic planning resulted in better coordination and greater unity.

Scheduling

Two practical tools that many churches have found to be very helpful are a church calendar and a schedule of events. The calendar used in our church is 24 inches by 36 inches and remains permanently displayed in the secretary's office. All major church events are placed on the calendar under her watchful eye. The church publishes and distributes a schedule of events to keep everyone abreast of events.

To summarize, strategic planning gives pastoral leaders an opportunity (1) to focus on their God-given ministries, (2) to remain sensitive to the leading of the Holy Spirit and the needs of those to whom God has called them to minister, (3) to anticipate and deal constructively with change, and (4) to better coordinate church activities. It can also help pastoral leaders to appreciate how God is working in their midst by causing them to stop and reflect upon how he has blessed the ministry. Now let's look at a simple approach to strategic planning.

AN APPROACH TO STRATEGIC PLANNING

If you were working in the corporate planning department of a major business and charged with the responsibility of developing your company's strategic plan, you would have to analyze extensively your firm's mission, market share, competitive position, strengths and weaknesses, and the opportunities and threats facing your company. The process would necessitate your gathering reams of information and would take several months (although you might be working on facets of it year-round). When it was all over, you would present your boss a big black three-ring notebook filled with pearls of wisdom and tactics guaranteed to vault your company over the heads of its competitors.

Many large Christian organizations (for example, mission boards, relief agencies, educational institutions, and megachurches) have successfully adopted similar planning processes. Their size and the complexity of their operations force them to do so. But few churches can justify the expense of extensive analyses. Nor is such a heavy quantitative approach necessary.[8] What then are the issues pastoral leaders need to deal with when they strategically plan for their church? Of course, no one approach to strategic planning will work best for all churches in all situations because every church is unique. The following approach does, however, provide a general framework that will help pastoral leaders discern the most important issues they need to address and provides a sound basis for planning and decision making.

STEP 1: STATE THE MISSION OF YOUR CHURCH

If your church's pastoral leaders have already thought through the issues raised in chapter 4, "Mission: The Purpose of the Local Church," this step will be easy. It is, however, important that you continually reaffirm your commitment to your church's mission (for example, worship, edification, and evangelism). This is especially important if you have new board members, since there are a number of factors influencing a church's mission (fig. 10-1). Everyone needs to be working with the same charter.

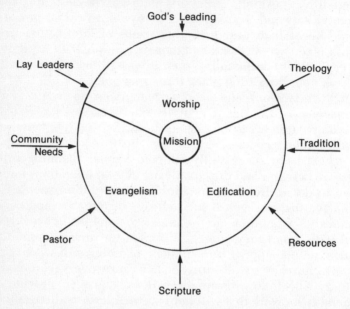

Figure 10-1
Factors Influencing a Church's Mission

If, on the other hand, you have never defined the mission of your church, it may be necessary for you to roll up your sleeves and do some serious reading, studying, and praying until you develop a consensus on the matter. The first question you must be able to answer clearly is, "What is the mission of our church?" Without a clear-cut concept of why the church exists, it will be difficult to formulate appropriate plans and objectives and almost impossible to impart a sense of vision to church members.[9]

Determining the Scope of Your Ministry

One of my best friends has a plaque hanging over his desk at work advising, "Know Thy Niche." It reminds him to make sure that he is working in the areas for which he is responsible and helps him to be more productive.

Do you know to whom God has called your church to minister? Many pastors assume they are simply responsible to minister to "whomever walks through the door." For the most part, it has been acceptable for churches to operate that way, and a church should openly receive and serve anyone who enters. But few churches can afford to be all things to all people. Many that try to do so perform many tasks poorly and miss unique ministry opportunities.

For example, when our church was established several years ago, the founding fathers believed that God had called them to create a nontraditional, body-life church that would reach people living in Highland Park and University Park (the "Park Cities"). The Park Cities is one of Dallas's oldest and wealthiest areas. It is also home to some outstanding churches, such as Highland Park Presbyterian Church, Highland Park Methodist Church, and Park Cities Baptist Church.

Three years after the church was founded, the elders conducted a church survey and discovered that less than 5 percent of the congregation lived in the Park Cities. Over 60 percent of the church was less than thirty years old. More than 70 percent had to drive over fifteen minutes to get to church. In short, instead of being a "neighborhood church," we were a regional church, with people attending from all over Dallas. We were also ministering to a very young population.

Gathering and evaluating this information was invaluable to us as we tried to discern the mission for our body of believers. Surveys can be an indispensable tool for any church, providing data for decision making. Appendix B is a thorough discussion of designing and distributing surveys. I heartily recommend the process to any church.

My church's survey showed that the issue the elders had to resolve was whether God had called them to develop a neighborhood church, primarily serving the Park Cities, or a regional church, serving people from all over Dallas. If it was the former, we needed to develop programs that would attract people from the Park Cities and minister to their needs.

After a substantial amount of discussion and prayer, the

elders concluded that Fellowship Bible Church of Park Cities should continue as a regional church, and it should not radically change its current ministries to reach the Park Cities. There were several good churches in the Park Cities already, and the elders sensed that God had "changed their marching orders." Moreover, we consciously recognized that, in comparison to other churches, our church would always attract a lot of young people because of our music, singles ministry, and informal worship.

Deciding we were a regional and not a neighborhood church was a major step that enabled us to clarify our mission.[10] It did not, however, preclude us from ministering to unique target groups or "niches." For example, one of our small groups adopted a refuge family from Cambodia, and a number of church members have been involved in good works throughout the city.

Consider the Needs

Figure 10-2 shows the major ministry subgroups at our church. Not all groups have the same characteristics or needs. One of the mistakes pastoral leaders frequently make is that they tend to treat everyone the same and fail to recognize that needs may change over time.

To put it simply, different populations have different needs. For example, self-image, identity, dating, and sexuality are big issues for young people. Adults may be more interested in raising healthy children. No single individual can grasp the unique characteristics and needs of each group. Therefore, whoever is primarily responsible for overseeing a particular subgroup should continually think through the particular needs of that group. Most of the information needed can be gathered by simply being out "among the people." To use a biblical analogy, shepherds are always with their sheep (Psalm 23).

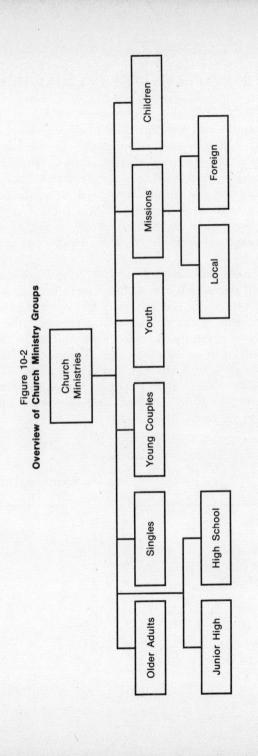

Figure 10-2
Overview of Church Ministry Groups

STEP 2: EVALUATE CURRENT MINISTRIES

One phenomenon that continues to amaze me is how quickly programs and services multiply in the local church. Even elders who are actively involved in the life of the church cannot fully grasp all that transpires. Therefore, it is helpful to review ministries on a regular basis. Some of this oversight function can be accomplished at regularly scheduled board meetings. It is also helpful to look at the big picture at least once or twice a year to see if ongoing ministries need to be modified or deleted, or if new ones need to be added.

For example, once a year we list our current ministries (fig. 10-3) and ask ourselves how they can be modified to meet better the needs of our congregation. Occasionally, decisions are made to end certain programs. For example, the church used to sponsor quarterly "Leadership Potlucks" on Wednesday nights. They were originally established as a means to communicate directly with key pastoral leaders. After two years of mediocre attendance, the elders concluded they were not ministering to people's needs and decided to drop the meetings—to no one's dismay.

Figure 10-3
Church Programs and Services

Program/Service	A	S	YC	Y	C	M
Worship Services	X	X	X			
Small Groups	X	X	X			
Discipleship Groups	X	X	X			
Biblical Studies Institute	X	X	X			
Counseling Services	X	X	X			
Couples Class	X	X	X			
Singles Class		X				
Mom-to-Mom			X			
Sunday School				X	X	
Vacation Bible School				X	X	

Target Group

124

Adopt-a-Missionary			X	X	X	X	X	X

*A = Adults	S = Singles	YC = Young Couples
Y = Youth	C = Children	M = Missions

At the same time, we pray about some of the ministries not being offered and try to discern whether the Lord would have us work in a new area. People in the body often prompt us to consider new areas. For example, for years the church provided little in the way of counseling and did not have a church newspaper. During one of our annual reviews, the elders sensed God's leading in these areas and decided to establish both. As of yet, however, the church has not developed special ministries for single parents, and except for the adoption of a Cambodian refugee family and the spontaneous efforts of church members, little has been done to facilitate social outreach.

STEP 3: DEVELOP GOALS AND OBJECTIVES

Once you have taken a good look at your portfolio of ministries, you are in a position to develop some goals and objectives for things you would like to accomplish during the coming year (or whatever time period under consideration).

The terms "goals," "objectives," and "action plans" are used repeatedly in management books but often with different meanings. To avoid confusion, let us define them as follows.

Goals

Goals may be defined as "the object or end that one strives to attain." A goal is usually something you want to accomplish long-term. For example, after reviewing current ministries and the needs of the body, Trinity's elders developed three major goals: (1) to build a new sanctuary, (2) to establish a ministry to couples, and (3) to improve communication within the body. One of the biggest mistakes pastoral leaders make when they first get serious about strategic planning is that they establish far too many goals. Conversely, one of the major characteristics of effective business managers is that they focus their time and energy on three or four major goals.[11]

Objectives

An objective is "a specific aim or result that is desired." For example, one of the objectives developed in conjunction with the goal of improving church communication was: "To publish a church newsletter three times a year." Well-written objectives have three characteristics: (1) they start with an action verb/infinitive (to publish), (2) they state a specific measurable result (a newsletter), and (3) they state a completion date or the frequency with which something is to be done (three times a year).

Peter Drucker is largely responsible for coining the phrase and developing the concept of "management by objectives" over thirty years ago.[12] When utilized in major corporations, managers and subordinates spend hours together developing objectives and evaluating progress. Although such a process can be quite productive, it is seldom necessary or feasible in the church. Nevertheless, objectives serve several valuable functions. In addition to guiding and directing behavior, they significantly influence the structure of an organization and relationships among members.

Action Plans

Action plans are "the actual, definitive steps taken to achieve an objective." For example, to publish a church newsletter one would have to take the following steps: (1) write or solicit articles, (2) print the letter, and (3) mail the letter. When developing action plans, Ted Engstrom and Edward Dayton (the "deans of Christian management") have observed that "no real *detail* planning is accurate beyond three months."[13] More will be said about action plans in the next chapter. What is important to remember at this point is that objectives state desired results; action plans state the steps leading to those results (fig. 10-4).

To repeat an earlier point, one of the biggest mistakes that novice strategic planners make in the planning process is that they go overboard with the number of goals and objectives they develop. By all means, be sensitive to the leading of the Holy Spirit, but also try to be realistic and to think about the "big picture." When you have completed your major goals and objectives, prioritize them so that the most important jobs are sure to be accomplished.

STEP 4: ASSIGN RESPONSIBILITIES

Developing goals and objectives is futile unless you assign someone to be responsible for implementing the objectives.[14] Unfortunately, this step in the planning process is often omitted (which is why a lot of goals and objectives never come to fruition). Here's an example.

Figure 10-4
Goals, Objectives, and Action Plans

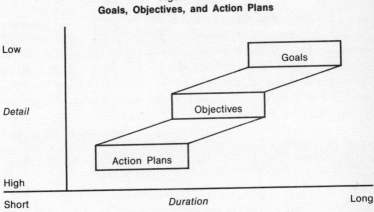

When Trinity decided to build a new sanctuary, one elder was assigned the overall responsibility for seeing that the job was accomplished. He, of course, received help from other people in the church, and he was free to go about the task any way he wanted. But in the final analysis, the responsibility was his. Had the task been delegated to a group of people, the building would have never been completed.

STEP 5: ESTABLISH A REVIEW SYSTEM

Once responsibilities have been assigned, it is important to establish some mechanism for monitoring progress. Otherwise, projects may not be completed. Accountability encourages a sense of responsibility. It is simply a fact of human nature that most people perform better when they know what is expected of them, when it is due, and that they will be held accountable for results. If the goal is something major, such as building a new sanctuary, pastoral leaders may decide it is necessary to have a weekly report from the person in charge. If the objective is something less ambitious, like publishing a church newspaper, a quarterly update may suffice.

SUMMARY

Churches will always differ in their approach to strategic planning. Smaller churches are more likely to use a less formal approach and communicate plans in person instead of in writing. In larger churches, the process is more likely to be formalized, especially if it gains the support of key pastoral leaders. Regardless of the approach, good strategic planning enables pastoral leaders to do a better job of providing the sheep under their care with a sense of direction and purpose (see fig. 10-5).

Figure 10-5
Overview of the Strategic Planning Process

Step 1: State the mission of the church
Step 2: Evaluate current ministries
Step 3: Develop goals and objectives
Step 4: Assign responsibilities
Step 5: Establish a review system

PRACTICAL SUGGESTIONS

Be Realistic

Strategic planning will not enable pastoral leaders to walk on water, nor will it solve every problem a church faces. Rather, it is a helpful way to think about the ministry and one's responsibilities so that the mission of the church can be accomplished.

Appoint a Coordinator

To see that the process is completed in a timely manner, consider assigning one individual responsibility for coordinating the church's strategic planning. The individual selected must be well-known and widely respected in the church. This person should also be closely involved in the life of the church, have an abundance of patience, and excellent people skills. Nonstaff board members are frequently ideal candidates because they are in a good position to be objective about the process. Remember, if everyone is responsible, no one is accountable.

Keep it Simple

My personal motto is "the simpler the better." It just doesn't make sense to get carried away with complex planning tomes. The basks of the ministry are pretty simple. What you want to strive for is a unified sense of purpose and a general strategy for accomplishing it. If you have time to spare and want to go into greater detail, then listing the church's strengths and weaknesses, opportunities and threats, etc., may be helpful. But do not let it derail you!

Review Ministries Regularly

When something has been neglected or reaches a crisis point, it is tempting to deal with it exhaustively (which is excruciating). One way to avoid that temptation is to make strategic planning a regular part of your ministry. When I was responsible for our church's planning, we used to meet twice a year on Saturday mornings to plan and discuss key issues. We also had ministry progress reports at regularly scheduled board meetings. The way it usually worked was that every month, a staff member (or the responsible party) would update the elders on an area of ministry (for example, singles) and share the plans for the coming months. The elders were available for input, but each person was responsible for developing the plans for his/her ministry and was free to pursue it as the Lord led. This allowed the elders to focus on issues/programs that affected the entire church, such as worship services.

Solicit the Thinking of Church Members

It simply does not make sense to ignore or neglect the input of church members. Two brains are always better than one. This does not mean that everyone in the congregation has to be surveyed before a decision can be made, but the viewpoints of representatives from each major ministry group should be solicited. This will also enable pastoral leaders to obtain a higher degree of goal ownership.

Communicate

I'm sure it's obvious that I am a strong advocate of communication. Thoughts and emotions need to be expressed. We all need to help each other understand our mutual vision for the church—verbally and in writing. After all, we are one body.

Never Stop Depending on God

Planning is good stewardship, but it is not a substitute for trusting God and prayer. As the apostle James illustrated, it is ridiculous to plan without submitting to God's will (James

4:11–13). As with all ministry endeavors, we need his grace, strength, and wisdom. So as we plan let us petition our powerful and loving God.

NOTES

1. Garry Friesen with J. Robin Maxson, *Decision Making and the Will of God* (Portland, Oreg.: Multnomah, 1982), 209–218.

2. C. Peter Wagner, *Strategies For Church Growth* (Ventura, Calif.: Regal, 1987), 17–34.

3. Daniel H. Gray, "Uses and Misuses of Strategic Planning," *Harvard Business Review* (January–February 1986): 89–97.

4. Amar Bhide, "Hustle As Strategy," *Harvard Business Review* (September–October 1986): 59–65.

5. Robert H. Schuller, *Your Church Has a Fantastic Future!* (Garden Grove, Calif.: Gospel Light, 1987), 252–54.

6. Thomas J. Peters and Robert H. Waterman, Jr., *In Search of Excellence* (New York: Harper & Row, 1982), 160–77.

7. Craig Hickman and Michael Silva, *Creating Excellence* (New York: NAC Books, 1984), 177–95.

8. Robert H. Hayes, "Strategic Planning—Forward in Reverse?" *Harvard Business Review* (November–December 1985): 111–19.

9. Warren Bennis and Burt Nanus, *Leaders: The Strategies for Taking Charge* (New York: Harper & Row, 1985), 88–93.

10. Philip Kotler, *Principles of Marketing* (Englewood Cliffs, N.J.: Prentice-Hall, 1980), 74–76.

11. H. Edward Wrapp, "Good Managers Don't Make Policy Decisions," *Harvard Business Review* (July–August 1984): 8–21.

12. Don Hellriegel and JS¾⅛York: West, 1983), 566–68.

13. Ted W. Engstrom and Edward R. Dayton, eds., "A Long Range Planning Context," *Christian Leadership Letter* (February 1987): 1–3.

14. James A. F. Stoner, *Management* (Englewood Cliffs, N.J.: Prentice-Hall, 1978), 112–60.

Chapter 11

Administration and Delegation: Plague or Promise?

> No leader can lead without delegating responsibilities to others, and perhaps there is no more delicate test of good leadership than the way in which leaders handle this task.
>
> John White
> *Excellence in Ministry*

The concept of administration is misunderstood in most Christian circles. Many Christians see it as an avalanche of detailed tasks. Making coffee, printing the bulletin, paying bills, writing letters, making phone calls and recruiting volunteers—what Eugene Peterson refers to as the "nuts and bolts" of running a church—are seen as defining the full scope of administration. Many pastoral leaders prefer to delegate this "administration" to deacons and deaconesses. Doing this presumably frees the leaders to focus on "real pastoral ministries," such as preaching, teaching, and counseling.

Some of these same people have even built an entire "theology of administration" on the basis of a single word used only once in the New Testament.[1] The word, *kyberneseis*, appears in 1 Corinthians 12:28 (the teaching on spiritual gifts), and has been translated "administrations" (NIV, NASB), "direction" (NEB), and "governments" (KJV).

But building an extensive theology on one verse (let alone one word) is both questionable and unnecessary. It also fails to convey the full import of the concept.

The meaning of "administration" has a greater span of applications then this narrow view allows. Michael Dibelius has pointed out:

> The position of kyberneseis after the gifts of healing and giving help, and before those of tongues, suggests that the word is a term for mediating function of keeping order within the whole life of the church.[2]

In other words, this particular spiritual gift is not primarily concerned with the details everyone wants to avoid. As C. K. Barrett explains in his penetrating commentary on 1 Corinthians, the term is used metaphorically and usually refers to the "steering of a ship."[3] Leon Morris states, "the function is obviously one of direction, and may be the work of elders. But we have no way of knowing."[4] Kittel draws the same conclusion.[5]

THE "GIFT" OF ADMINISTRATION

Two inferences are in order. First, the gift of administration probably refers to the process of providing wise "direction" and "oversignt" in pastoral matters. Second, as Thomas Campbell persuasively argues, it is most likely a fairly common, widely distributed gift. It is incorrect then, to assume that the gift of administration is limited to elders or that it is the only gift a person can have.[6]

Carl F. George, director of the Charles E. Fuller Institute

of Evangelism and Church Growth, believes that the "essence of the administrative gift is the ability to recognize ability." Some people find it easy to establish goals and visualize what is required to accomplish them.[7] And as Ray S. Anderson points out in his book *Minding God's Business*, it is a gift which many Christian leaders have, along with gifts of exhortation, faith, and stewardship.[8] Paul's leadership in raising funds to support the poor in the church at Jerusalem is a classic illustration of the gift of administration at work: his task involved organizing people in various parts of the world in order for the project to succeed (2 Corinthians 8:16–19).

Taking care of bothersome details does not capture the essence of the gift of administration. The point is this: it is unwise to assume that God has blessed your church with one individual who wants to make "details" or "mundane matters" his/her life's work. Some people may be more task-oriented by nature and find it easy to get things done, but if a church is going to function in a healthy manner, everyone needs to shoulder a portion of the details. Delegating such details (or anything else), however, is often difficult.

BARRIERS TO DELEGATION

Perfectionism

Pastoral leaders (as well as business managers) fail to delegate for a variety of reasons. One of the biggest barriers is perfectionism; many pastoral leaders are simply afraid that others cannot or will not do a job properly. This was a problem that plagued John at Trinity. Even though the church had several capable teachers, the only time he voluntarily surrendered the pulpit on Sundays was when he was out of town. John's reticence to trust others with preaching at worship services did not stem from the fact that he was a spellbinding preacher or that other lay leaders were not interested in preaching. He was simply afraid that something might go wrong on Sunday morning and that visitors might not return.

Although John's fears were exaggerated, they were not totally groundless. One church leader had once delivered a terribly boring sermon. But few people expect to hear a "perfect" sermon every Sunday, and most enjoy listening to a lay person once in a while. In short, pastoral leaders who subscribe to the adage, "If you want something done right, do it yourself," find delegation difficult.

Fear of Losing Power and Authority

Another barrier to delegation is the pastoral leaders' fear (conscious or unconscious) that they will lose some of their power and authority if and when others do something well (or better than they do). For example, Tom was not a particularly gifted musician, but during a time when he was feeling discouraged and insecure, he resisted relinquishing responsibility for leading the singing to a layman who was much more qualified. Fortunately, Mary helped Tom to realize what he was doing, and he delegated the task. As a result, the musician's spiritual gifts were utilized for the benefit of the body, and Tom was free to devote himself to responsibilities genuinely enjoyed.

Lack of Ability

A third reason why many pastoral leaders fail to delegate is a lack of ability to do so. Simply stated, many people are too disorganized and overwhelmed with daily responsibilities to take the time needed to delegate. The good news is that with a little discipline and practice, everyone can learn to delegate effectively.

Reluctance to Accept Responsibility

A fourth reason for not delegating is that people are often reluctant to accept responsibility. For example, when the elders at Trinity tried to find new elders, most candidates declined because they felt they needed additional training or were not qualified. In addition, many lay people shy away from accepting new responsibilities because they are afraid they will be criticized for doing less than a perfect job. This is an especially disheartening reason to drop out of the race because the only way one can develop gifts and ministry skills is to exercise them. The solution to this problem is (1) to assure people that "mistakes" are a normal part of the learning process, (2) to affirm them whenever they minister, and (3) to provide whatever training is needed to develop confidence in potential leaders' ability to minister.

ADVANTAGES OF DELEGATION

Shared Responsibility

Given the fairly extensive barriers to delegation, it is easy to understand why so many well-meaning pastoral leaders like John become tied to duties they do not like (such as overseeing church finances). John took the attitude "someone's got to do it." Certainly I agree that as a result of the Fall, everyone has to do things they do not like. That is just a part of life. But when 10 percent of the church does 90 percent of the ministry, the body deteriorates.

No body part should be allowed to atrophy. Perhaps, then, the most cogent argument for delegation is that it encourages others to accept responsibility, and thereby exercise their spiritual gifts. The whole body of Christ is subsequently strengthened.

Of course, more participation requires better organization. For all believers to be doing their part in the church, pastoral leaders need to learn how to better organize other people. Often leaders do not know how to orchestrate tasks or even meetings to maximize the use of others' skills and minimize the expenditure of their time. This can be pivotal in maintaining enthusiasm for participation in any given project. Appendix C delineates key elements to leading a productive meeting, providing specific suggestions for pastoral leaders. A well-run meeting is both a prerequisite to and an advantageous result of proper delegation.

Better Decisions, More Meaningful Ministry

Another advantage of delegation is its contribution toward better decisions and more meaningful ministry.[9] For example, if the elders at Trinity had insisted on maintaining total control of every aspect of the church's building program, the new sanctuary might never have been completed. Assigning one elder primary responsibility to coordinate the project and act as a liaison with the building committee enabled them to cut through a lot of time-consuming red tape.

Forming shepherding groups to oversee the church's small groups had a similar effect. It would have been virtually impossible for the designated staff person to meet the needs of every small-group leader personally. Each shepherding-group leader could, however, keep in touch with four or five other group leaders.

More Effective Oversight

Another advantage of delegation is that it enables pastoral leaders to engage in personal ministry and to deal effectively with their oversight responsibilities. For example, one reason why the elders at Trinity have stopped planning and lost their sense of direction is that they became overburdened with the day-to-day details of running the church. Ten percent of the congregation simply cannot meet the needs of the entire church!

PREREQUISITES TO EFFECTIVE DELEGATION

In many business corporations, before a manager delegates significant responsibilities, he or she is required to develop a comprehensive job description clearly outlining the nature of the task to be performed and the standards by which such performance will be evaluated. A number of major Christian organizations, like World Vision, find it helpful to engage in similar processes. The primary advantage of such an approach is that it forces one to think through exactly what needs to be accomplished. Such an approach is quite appropriate for major organizations and for positions that can be defined precisely and measured quantifiably.

However, as Thomas Campbell points outs, in many cases it would be better to avoid such a process in the local church so that everyone would realize that the pastor's role is subject to many interpretations and changes as the body (organism) develops.[10] Furthermore, developing an exhaustive job description does not, by itself, guarantee that projects will be completed on time. As anyone who has tried to delegate knows, nothing is more frustrating than to delegate a significant task only to have it left untouched or unfinished.

MANAGEMENT PROCESS, TASK CLARITY, AND ACTION PLANS

To prepare for writing this chapter, I read several books and articles and interviewed a number of pastoral leaders and business executives.[11] The issue I researched was simple: namely, what can be done to see that tasks are completed in a timely manner without being overbearing, manipulative, or provoking guilt? In the final analysis, it is really a fairly simple process (see fig. 11-1).

What: Task Clarity

First, as figure 11-1 indicates, pastoral leaders need to decide "What" it is that needs to be done. It's impossible to hit a bull's-eye if the target isn't set up first. Let's say the board of elders has just finished some strategic planning and has concluded that the church needs to develop a training program for small-group leaders. Such a program could encompass a variety of elements. So let's provide a specific example for illustrative purposes. Suppose the church wants to develop a small-group training program that will enable

Figure 11-1
Management Process and Task Clarity

Task Clarity	Management Process		
What (Task)	Who (Responsible Party)	When (Date to be Completed)	Personal Follow-up

Resources:

leaders to (1) lead inductive Bible studies, (2) facilitate personal sharing in a group, and (3) lead a group in prayer. Carefully articulating "What" needs to be accomplished is referred to by business managers as "task clarity."

Who: Responsible Party

Next we need to decide "Who" is going to be responsible for the "What" (for example, developing the training program). The process frequently breaks down at this point because instead of assigning one person ultimate responsibility for a project, a task is delegated to a group, which inevitably results in a lot of confusion about who is responsible for what. Let's say we assign Tom ultimate responsibility for the project. He knows that he can draw upon the resources of other believers in the body, and he can even delegate part of the task, but ultimately it is his responsibility to see that the task is accomplished. He is accountable (that is, answerable) for results.

When: Target Date for Completion

The third decision we need to make is to determine "When" the project needs to be completed. Sometimes it is difficult to know how long it will take to complete a task, but unless a specific target date for completion (and/or review) is established, the project can (and will) drag on indefinitely. As Pastor Don Baker has said, "If I plan to reach my goals, I must continually check my progress."[12] Establishing a completion date of the task/project under consideration is essential. Referring to the example, we could say that Tom's project should be completed by October 15.

To review, here is what we have done. We have decided (1) *What* needs to be done, (2) *Who* is ultimately responsible for seeing that the task is accomplished, and (3) *When* it is due. We need to set up a procedure to see that it all comes together. In figure 11-1 the fourth column, *Personal Follow-up*, represents that part of the progress. Using the example to illustrate, we could say that the elders would expect a progress report from Tom on September 15.

But What About the "How"?

If the task of developing a training program for small-group leaders has been delegated to Tom, then it is ultimately his responsibility to decide "How" to do it. If it is an area others know something about, Tom may want to solicit their input, and others should feel free to offer suggestions. But in the final analysis, Tom is the one who, with God's grace, has to see that the task is completed. Ted Engstrom states in *Your Gift of Administration* that "a key word in the delegation process is the word entrust.[13] Individuals must be trusted. It is the only way they will develop their own gifts and abilities.

In 2 Timothy 2:1–2, Paul writes,

> You then, my son, be strong in the grace that is in Christ Jesus. And the things you have heard me say in the presence of many witnesses entrust to reliable men who will also be qualified to teach others.

Paul knew Timothy's strengths and weaknesses. He was well aware of Timothy's tendency to be shy (2 Timothy 1:6–7), but Paul trained him, challenged him, and trusted him with significant ministry responsibilities. He did not give Timothy step-by-step instructions on how to accomplish his tasks. He left the specifics of "how" up to Timothy.

Action Plans

In other words, Timothy was free to develop his own plan of action. Some people like to make long lists and plan agendas down to the smallest detail. Others prefer to go about their business more intuitively; they "feel" their way along. As long as the work is done in a manner which pleases the Lord (2 Corinthians 5:9), the approach does not matter.

John W. Slocum, past president of the American Academy of Management, has written, "The most basic requirement for effective delegation is the willingness by managers to give their subordinates real freedom to accomplish delegated tasks."[14] Goals and objectives developed by pastoral leaders under the guidance of the Holy Spirit do not justify the use of unbiblical or worldly "means" to accomplish them, but the process does not have to be micro-, managed by board members. Ray Anderson has said, "An action plan is viable only for as long as the assumptions that called for it are valued."[15]

God may guide pastoral leaders to modify a course of action drastically. More frequently, the individual(s) responsible for a particular project have to make mid-course adjustments. Therefore, a person often needs flexibility with details to remain faithful to the overall vision for the project.

Accountability and Administrative Style

Delegation and administration frequently disintegrate (especially in nonprofit organizations) because few people relish someone "checking up" on them. It makes most of us feel uncomfortable. A contributing factor, of course, is that many people fear failure and dislike criticism. Furthermore, the nature of "volunteer" work itself seems to run counter to the administrative process discussed earlier (for example, "Since I'm not getting paid, any level of performance is okay.").

Being evaluated is threatening, certainly. But evaluating someone else is also risky. After all, no one wants to be thought of as overbearing or dominating the progress of a particular project. In short, accountability can be difficult for everyone.[16] The fact that the church is almost totally dependent on "volunteers" for its support makes matters even more complicated. It is no wonder that many tasks are never accomplished.

So how are leaders to deal with the dilemma? They need an abundance of grace and patience (1 Peter 5:1–4). It's damaging to use authority as a threat. Remember the church is not IBM. Setting up a tightly structured management control system is not appropriate. But graciously following up on the status of a project does not have to be threatening for anyone. As G. K. Chesterton says, "We're all in the same boat, in a stormy sea, and we owe each other a terrible loyalty." Most church members who are given significant responsibilities and the authority to accomplish them will not resist being held accountable or respond defensively as long as they are (1) dealt with graciously, and (2) not given more than they can handle. This is especially true when they sense that pastoral leaders are sensitive to the leading of the Holy Spirit and fervent in prayer.

But Is All This Really Spiritual?

"To see a need or even to define an objective," says Pastor Don Baker, "solves nothing. Action is required."[17] The issues discussed in this chapter can assist pastoral leaders to overcome their resistance to delegation and enable them to take effective action. This can result in a living legacy of accomplished good works (Matthew 5:16).

Nevertheless, well-meaning Christians will invariably raise questions about the "spirituality" of the process. Ray Anderson wrestles with this subject at length in the insightful *Minding God's Business*. In his chapter entitled "But Is All This Really Spiritual?" Anderson concludes that the only way to counter such doubts is (1) to show from Scripture how Christ and the apostles planned and carried out their actions; and (2) to make sure that one's own style reflects a sensitivity to the leading and empowering of the Holy Spirit (Acts 1:8), dependence on prayer in the planning process (instead of seeing the planning as the guaranty of the success of actions), and confidence in the sovereignty of God.[18] The corporate culture of a community of believers should be very different than that of a Fortune 500 company, especially in the area of administration and delegation. Otherwise, the promise becomes a plague.

143

Figure 11-2
Volunteer Viewpoint

If you want my loyalty, interests and best efforts, remember that . . .

1. I need a *sense of belonging,* a feeling that I am honestly needed for my total self, not just for my hands nor because I take orders well.

2. I need to have a sense of sharing in planning our objectives. My need will be satisfied only when I feel that *my* ideas have had a fair hearing.

3. I need to feel that the goals and objectives arrived at are *within* reach and that they make sense to *me.*

4. I need to feel that what I'm doing has *real purpose* or contributes to human welfare—that its value extends even beyond my personal gain or my time.

5. I need to share in *making the rules* by which together we shall live and work toward our goals.

6. I need to know in some clear detail just what is expected of me—not only my detailed task, but where I have opportunity to make personal and final decisions.

7. I need to have some *responsibilities that challenge,* that are within range of my abilities and interest, that contribute toward reaching my assigned goal, and that advance all the goals.

8. I need to *see* that *progress* is being made toward the goals we have set.

9. I need to be kept informed. What I'm not *up* on, I may be *down* on. (Keeping me informed is one way to give me status as in individual.)

10. I need to have confidence in my superiors—confidence based on assurance of consistently fair treatment, recognition when it is due, and trust that loyalty will bring increased security.

In brief, it really doesn't matter how much sense *my part* in this organization makes to *you*—I must feel that the whole deal makes sense to me!

Source: Harriet Naylor, *Volunteers Today: Finding, Training, and Working With Them* (New York: Dryden Associates, 1967, 1973), 18–19.

NOTES

1. Walter Bauer, *A Greek-English Lexicon of the New Testament and Other Early Christian Literature*, trans. W. F. Arndt and F. W. Gingrich (Chicago: University of Chicago Press, 1957), 457.
2. Colin Brown, ed., *Dictionary of New Testament Theology*, vol. 1 (Grand Rapids: Zondervan, 1975), 198–99.
3. C. K. Barrett, *The First Epistle to the Corinthians* (New York: Harper & Row, 1968), 295.
4. Leon Morris, *The First Epistle of Paul to the Corinthians* (Grand Rapids: Eerdmans, 1976), 179.

5. Gerhard Kittel and Gerhard Friedrich, eds., *Theological Dictionary of the New Testament*, trans. Geoffrey W. Bromiley, vol. 3 (Grand Rapids: Eerdmans, 1965), 250.

6. Ted W. Engstrom, *Your Gift of Administration: How to Discover and Use It* (Nashville: Thomas Nelson, 1983), 21–34.

7. Carl F. George, "Recruitment's Missing Link," *Leadership* (Summer 1982): 54–59.

8. Ray S. Anderson, *Minding God's Business* (Grand Rapids: Eerdmans, 1986), 72–77.

9. Don Hellriegel and John W. Slocum, Jr., *Management* (New York: Addison-Wesley, 1986), 350–65.

10. Thomas C. Campbell and Gary B. Reierson, *The Gift of Administration* (Philadelphia: Westminster Press, 1981), 40.

11. James Anderson and Ezra Jones, *The Management of the Ministry* (New York: Harper & Row, 1986), 142–55.

12. Don Baker, *Leadership* (Portland, Oreg.: Multnomah, 1985), 22.

13. Engstrom, *Your Gift of Administration*, 52.

14. Hellriegel and Slocum, *Management*, 99.

15. Anderson and Jones, *The Management of the Ministry*, 83.

16. Robert H. Schaffer, "Demand Better Results—and Get Them," *Harvard Business Review* (November–December 1974): 91–98.

17. Baker, *Leadership*, 11.

18. Anderson and Jones, *The Management of the Ministry*, 125–43.

Chapter 12

Financial Stewardship: Managing Church Finances

It is required of stewards that one be found trustworthy.

(1 Corinthians 4:2 NASB)

If you haven't got financial integrity, you haven't got a message to proclaim.[1]

Stan Allaby, Pastor
Black Rock Congregational Church

In the first part of 1987, revelations of the personal misconduct and gross financial mismanagement at the PTL Club stunned Americans. All the major newspapers and television networks told the story. Hollywood's most creative writers could not have developed a script more embarrassing to the evangelical community. Yet, if adultery had been the only misdeed involved, Jim Bakker might have been able to remain the head of the PTL ministry. Misusing money raised to further the Lord's work is another matter. The lack of

146

financial controls and the poor monetary stewardship that were disclosed in subsequent investigations were shocking to many Christians and non-Christians alike.

No one knows the long-term results of the PTL controversy, but the short-term consequences are certain: (1) a number of faithful supporters stopped giving, (2) the credibility of evangelical Christianity in general, and TV ministries in particular, was called into question, and (3) the PTL ministry filed for bankruptcy.[2] There was also the threat of PTL's losing its nonprofit status, pending investigation by the Internal Revenue Service (IRS).[3]

THE NEED FOR PLANNING, POLICIES AND PROCEDURES

Fortunately, the finances of most churches are managed much more responsibly than the PTL Club. What problems do emerge are usually of a much different nature and do not result from greed or the abuse of power. In fact, most of the financial stewardship problems that develop in local church ministries are due to (1) poor planning, or the lack of any planning, and (2) a failure to establish basic policies and procedures regarding church finances.

One of the most blatant illustrations of Trinity's failure to plan properly was when it was notified by the bank that a $7,500 interest payment was delinquent. The sum of $7,500 may be insignificant to some organizations, but it was a large sum for Trinity. The elders were thoroughly embarrassed and their credibility was damaged when they were forced to make several "crisis" pleas for money to the congregation.

A less obvious, but equally serious, failure to plan was demonstrated annually by the manner in which staff pay increases were handled. Here is what usually happened. Around Christmas time, when everyone had an extra measure of goodwill, the elders would conclude that something needed to be done about staff salaries. No one had any idea about salaries for other ministers in the area, nor had anyone devised a philosophy of compensation. Most of the time one elder would suggest a certain percentage raise for all, usually based on the rate of inflation. Another would counter with a different percentage, then they would compromise.

Of course, the main factor guiding the amount of staff raises was the church's balance at the bank. If money was tight, raises were small. If the church was flush with cash, raises were large. The nature of a person's responsibilities, performance, or length of service had little to do with the amount of the raise.

Failing to establish basic policies and procedures with respect to how money would be handled created even greater problems. For example, it was not uncommon for the senior pastor or one of the ushers to count the offering alone. This violated one of the basic principles of prudent cash management: two people should always count the cash together.[4]

Trinity also violated the IRS prohibition against designated giving. For example, they allowed one of the church's more wealthy couples to establish an "educational fund" at the church to pay for their nephew's theological training. Through this, the couple received the full tax benefits of their "donation" as they helped finance their nephew's education. The elders also allowed several businessmen to establish a special "church" fund and raise money so that one of the church's staff members could move to a beautiful home in a very nice part of town.

Although these actions reflected a genuine concern for and appreciation of the persons involved, both were against the law. The latter was also unfair because it violated one of the fundamental tenets of salary administration: internal equity. Everyone needs to be treated fairly. Tom and Mary, who had several small children and lived in a lower-class neighborhood, received no such help.

Situations like these can be avoided by adhering to the law of the land (Romans 13:1–7), by following principles set forth by the Evangelical Council for Financial Accountability (ECFA), and by establishing basic policies and procedures for handling church finances (fig. 12-1).[5]

Figure 12-1
ECFA's Seven Standards of Responsible Stewardship

1. Every member organization shall subscribe to a written statement of faith clearly affirming its commitment to the evangelical Christian faith and shall conduct its financial operations in a manner which reflects generally accepted Christian practices.

2. Every member organization shall be governed by a responsible board, a majority of whom shall not be employees/staff, and/or related by blood or marriage, which shall meet at least semiannually to establish policy and review its accomplishments.

3. Every member organization shall obtain an annual audit performed by an independent public accounting firm in accordance with generally accepted auditing standards (GAAS) with financial statements prepared in accordance with generally accepted accounting principles (GAAP).

4. Every member organization shall have a functioning audit review committee appointed by the board, a majority of whom shall not be employees/staff, and/or related by blood or marriage, for the purpose of reviewing the annual audit and reporting its findings to the board.

5. Every member organization shall provide a copy of its current audited financial statements upon written request.

6. Every member organization shall conduct its activities with the highest standards of financial integrity.

7. Every member organization shall comply with each of the ECFA standards for fund-raising.

Source: Evangelical Council for Financial Accountability. Reprinted by permission.

GUIDELINES FOR PASTORAL LEADERS

No single set of policies and procedures applies to all churches; every church is unique. Nevertheless, most pastoral leaders would profit by considering the following.

Teach Principles of Stewardship

The Bible is not silent on matters of stewardship and money.[6] Indeed, the Lord spent a great deal of time on these subjects (Matthew 17:24–27; Mark 12:41–44). Unfortunately, many churches treat the subject of money like sex and refuse to discuss it. It's crucial, however, for every Christian to understand the role of money and the basics of good stewardship (1 Corinthians 9).

Carefully Evaluate the Role of the Senior Pastor

A major reason why churches experience problems of financial management is that the senior pastor becomes the chief financial officer, head fund-raiser, and bookkeeper. It is remarkable how many pastors, who vigorously eschew other organizational tasks because they do not have administrative gifts, become heavily involved in the day-to-day administrative details of raising money, budgeting, and paying bills.

Some pastors do so by default, because no one else will do the job. (That was what happened to John at Trinity.) Other pastors feel strongly that they "need" to know what is going on. In still other cases board members may put pressure on the pastor to raise money, even though he may not want to and even though it may eventually compromise his ability to minister freely.

In the final analysis, these are issues that the pastoral leaders of every church must sort through for themselves. But I am reminded of what my college pastor once said in a message on relationships: "If you really love the girl you're dating, keep your hands off her." It is not that he thought it was wrong to be affectionate; he simply felt that accelerating physical activity in dating relationships inhibited in-depth communication and the development of healthy friendships.

So if you really love your pastor, tell him to keep his hands off the money. Don't let him become the chief fund-raiser and treasurer. Do not put him in situations that might cause others to question his motives or restrict his ability to minister freely. Both you and he will be glad you did!

Select Financial Stewards Carefully

Most churches form a finance committee that includes established business and professional people (such as bankers, lawyers, CPAs) to oversee church finances. For practical reasons, at least two elders or key pastoral leaders should be on the committee. In addition to facilitating communication between the board and the committee, this provides a healthy system of checks and balances.

Qualifications for membership on the committee and the nature of a committee member's responsibilities must be carefully spelled out—in writing. One should not assume that any successful (that is, rich) business person is qualified to be on the finance committee because many successful business people know little or nothing about the practical mechanics of establishing a budget or setting up financial control systems for nonprofit organizations.[7] It is absolutely essential that committee members be above reproach, trustworthy, and respected by those within and outside the church (1 Corinthians 4:2). They must continually keep the board/congregation informed about all financial matters.

Establish an Effective Control System

Like other organizations, churches operate in a dynamic environment. As a church grows and changes, its financial control systems must also change. Policies and procedures that become redundant, irrelevant, or ineffective must be eliminated. Other policies and procedures may need to be updated and new ones developed. Periodic review is essential in maintaining sound stewardship. In most churches, board members are ultimately responsible for seeing that the church's financial matters are handled with the greatest integrity.

ELEMENTS OF AN EFFECTIVE CONTROL SYSTEM

A control system is as effective as the sum of its parts. The elements of an effective control system include the following:

- Clearly defined responsibilities
- Clearly defined policies and procedures

151

- Segregation of duties
- Record keeping and information systems
- Budgets

What follows is a more thorough description of each of these parts.

Clearly Defined Responsibilities

All parties need to know their responsibilities and they need enough training and authority to fulfill their responsibilities. This is especially important in churches and other nonprofit organizations where volunteers are used for a variety of administrative tasks.

Policies and Procedures

The operating policies of an organization and its major accounting procedures for executing transactions must be clearly communicated to everyone involved in the process. These policies and procedures must be easily accessible to appropriate personnel. Although it takes a lot of work, written manuals are especially helpful when volunteers or part-time people are used.

Segregation of Duties

This may surprise some readers, but responsibilities should be assigned to people in such a manner that no individual controls all aspects of processing a financial transaction. For example, ushers who collect and count the offering should not be responsible for depositing the funds in the bank. Dividing work assignments helps to create a system of checks and balances that reduce the possibility that error, mismanagement, or fraud will go undetected.

Financial Stewardship: Managing Church Finances

Record Keeping and Information Systems

Information is a critical component of good financial stewardship. Accurate and timely information enables an organization to examine and verify past transactions and current levels of assets. The following records generally provide the information necessary for local churches:

- Cash receipts journal
- Cash disbursements journal
- Accounts receivable ledger
- Accounts payable ledger
- Payroll ledger
- Fixed asset ledger
- Investment ledger
- General journal
- General ledger

Financial Reporting System

A clear, concise, and timely report explaining important financial aspects of the church's operations should be developed and distributed on a regular basis to all church members. The benefit of such a report is that it helps to assure that money is handled appropriately and that transactions are reported accurately. For some strange reason, when it comes to disclosing information about church finances, a number of church leaders act as if they are the owners of a privately held corporation. Only a privileged few have access to important information, and it is rarely shared with the congregation. A major exception, of course, is the time someone gets a new "vision" for expanding operations (that is, building campaigns). At such points, many church leaders become surprisingly open and conversant about financial matters.

Budgets

Budgets are an essential element of good stewardship. They enable pastoral leaders to monitor the flow of resources in and out of the church. Comparing actual budgets with estimates often provides the first indication of operating problems or weaknesses in the church's financial control system. Three types of budgets are usually required: an operating budget, a cash-flow budget, and a capital budget.

An operating budget projects revenue and expenditures for one or more future periods. Forecasts are based on experience and educated assumptions about the future.

Cash-flow budgets estimate cash receipts and cash disbursements. They forecast cash balances at different intervals in the operating cycle.

Capital budgets specify future expenditures for capital acquisitions (that is, land, buildings, and equipment) that have been formally approved.

ON BEING ABOVE REPROACH

Many members of the clergy preach on the necessity for honesty and obedience to God's law. Some of these same individuals, however, personally ignore Paul's admonition to "submit to government" (Romans 13:8) and Christ's command to pay taxes (Matthew 24:8). People are surprised, disillusioned and discouraged when the fraud is exposed.

Obeying the letter of God's law in this matter is obviously critical. But obeying the spirit of God's law is equally important. (As an attorney friend puts it, "It is entirely possible to be lawful, but unethical.")

Somehow, many church leaders have become confused about the basics. They have taken black-and-white areas and smudged them into grey. The two areas where this is most prevalent are designated giving and fund-raising.

Designated Giving

The law says that a gift is tax deductible if (1) the group or organization receiving the gift is a *501(c)(3)* corporation, and (2) it is not earmarked for the benefit of a specific person or persons. The law is not vague. A church either does or does not have a tax-exempt status as a *501(c)(3)* corporation. A donation either is or is not earmarked to an organization or individual. If it is the latter, it is not tax deductible. To use

154

the church as a clearing agent (that is, to "launder" money) for a directed gift to an individual is an abuse of the church's tax-exempt status and a violation of the laws of God and the land.

Why, then, do churches fall into this trap? Some do it out of ignorance; they simply do not understand the law. Others do it because the IRS permits missions organizations to allow donors to earmark their gifts for specific missionaries. Most (if not all) missions organizations honor such requests as long as the donation is being used for legitimate ministry purposes. Pastoral leaders may also establish "benevolence funds" to channel resources to the needy, but the policies and procedures for handling such matters need to be clearly stated so that the system is not abused. The problem with Trinity's educational fund setup was that the couple were giving it directly to their nephew, a staff member. (Wouldn't everyone like to be able to deduct a family member's educational expenses?) The designated giving was not an "arm's length" transaction, nor was it a request. It was a stipulation.

Taking liberty with the law in that way can have far-reaching and devastating consequences. One result is that the church can lose its tax-exempt status. Equally debilitating for the church is that rationalizing one's way around the law tends to be generalized into other areas. The hidden message is that it's okay to bend the rules for the kingdom of God. Nothing could be further from the truth.

Fortunately, a number of evangelical leaders have become aware of the problem and are actively working to correct problems and abuses. The Evangelical Council for Financial Accountability, founded in 1974, has established "Seven Standards of Responsible Stewardship" for leaders of Christian organizations. More than 300 Christian organizations subscribe to the ECFA's statement of standards. Note especially the sixth statement indicated in figure 12-1 (p. 149): "Every member organization should conduct its activities with the highest standards of financial integrity." These standards are also supported by the "Donor's Bill of

Rights" (fig. 12-2). The imperative for believers, then, is to handle money in a manner that is above reproach.

Figure 12-2
Donor's Bill of Rights

Make sure your charity's standards and guidelines assure you a "bill of rights" as a donor. You have the right to:

1. Know how the funds of an organization are being spent.
2. Know what the programs you support are accomplishing.
3. Know that the organization is in compliance with federal, state, and municipal laws.
4. Restrict or designate your gifts to a particular project.
5. A response to your inquiries about finances and programs.
6. Visit offices and program sites of an organization to talk personally with the staff.
7. Not be high pressured into giving to any organization.
8. Know that the organization is well managed.
9. Know that there is a responsible governing board and who those board members are.
10. Know that all appeals for funds are truthful and accurate.

Source: Evangelical Council for Financial Accountability. Used by permission.

CHALLENGING ISSUES

At some point, every church will need to decide how church finances will be handled. Some decisions will be fairly simple: Will the plate be passed or not? Who'll count the money? Will donors be sent receipts?

Other decisions will be difficult to resolve. Three in particular tend to be troublesome: (1) the confidentiality of donations, (2) fund-raising methods, and (3) staff compensation. Space does not permit an extensive discussion of each matter, but a few comments are in order.

Confidentiality. Some churches go out of their way to give major donors significant positions in the church and high visibility. Such individuals frequently become part of the board, and the pastor almost always knows them by name and personally acknowledges their gift(s). Unless church leaders are very careful, wealthy members will unduly influence the direction of the church and garner an inordinate amount of the pastor's attention. They may also miss the blessing that comes from "private giving" (Matthew 7).

Fund-raising methods. It hurts to acknowledge it, but the fund-raising methods of some Christian organizations do not differ significantly from those of non-Christian organizations. Sometimes they are even worse. How money is raised or solicited is as important as how it is spent.[8]

Staff compensation. Next to the struggles a church faces with designated giving and periods when donations drop sharply (usually during the summer months), this is the area that gives pastoral leaders the most intense headaches.

By now, everyone agrees that the laborer is worthy of his wages (1 Timothy 5:18), but what is a fair wage? Is it determined by length of service? Education? Publications? Performance? Need? The average salary of church members?

Regardless of the specific guidelines a church uses to establish the level of its staff's compensation, pastoral leaders need to remember two things. First, the elements of compensation include direct benefits (the paycheck) and indirect benefits (the silent paycheck). The latter includes things like insurance benefits, housing allowances, travel expenses, educational funds, vacation time, and the freedom to set one's own hours. One of my accounting professors related that while he could earn much more money as a consultant or as a partner in a CPA firm, he felt that the freedom and flexibility of his profession (that is, the hidden paycheck), the intrinsic value of what he was doing, and job satisfaction were worth more than a bigger paycheck. That evaluation is not far different from the situation a pastor faces. Make sure staff members understand their total compensation package.

Pastoral leaders also need to remember the objectives of an effective compensation program. First, it must be fair to everyone on staff. An organization must maintain internal equity or bitter divisions will develop. Second, a sound compensation program should relieve staff members of financial worries so that they can focus on the ministry with single-mindedness. That does not mean, however, that every pastor has a right to expect the congregation to send his children to private schools. Nor does it mean that the church has an obligation to bail staff members out of bad investments. Staff people, like everyone else, need to trust God to provide for their needs. But a pastor's wife should not have to work to support the family simply because her husband is grossly underpaid.

RECLAIMING OUR HONOR

Many pastors are not trained in financial affairs. Gordon Loux, chairman of the executive committee of the Evangelical Council for Financial Accountability, made this startling statement: "In my four years of seminary, never once did I have a class on stewardship or managing church finances.[9] Unfortunately he is not alone.

In an article in a recent Christianity Today Institute forum titled "Reclaiming Our Honor," Kenneth Kantzer points out that the church will never be able to prevent financial scandals entirely. Nevertheless, Kantzer says that "we must begin by holding our leaders accountable for maintaining a life and ministry consistent with their profession." Clearly there's a need for seminaries to provide more training in the management of church finances.

NOTES

1. "Financial Facts of Life," *Leadership* (Winter 1987): 130–37.
2. "Bakker 'Covenants' Alleged," *Dallas Morning News*, 19 June 1987, 34.
3. "A Crackdown of PTL," *Christianity Today* (12 June 1987): 51–53.
4. *Effective Internal Accounting for Non-Profit Organizations: A Guide for Directors and Management* (New York: Price-Waterhouse, 1982), 9–10.

5. Further information is available from the Evangelical Council for Financial Accountability, P.O. Box 17511, Washington, DC 20041.

6. Colin Brown, ed., *Dictionary of New Testament Theology,* vol. 2 (Grand Rapids: Zondervan, 1975), 829–53.

7. Eugene B. Habecker, "Biblical Guidelines For Asking and Giving," *Christianity Today* (15 May 1987): 32.

8. Quentin J. Schultze, "Insiders Evaluate Evangelical Fundraising," *United Evangelical Action* (September–October 1986): 6–11. See also David L. McKenna, "Financing the Great Commission," *Christianity Today* (15 May 1987): 26–31.

9. "The Institute Talks to Fund Raisers," *Christianity Today* (15 May 1987): 35–40.

Chapter 13

Life Cycles: Stages in the Life of a Church

There is still much to learn about processes of development in organizations.[1]

Larry E. Greiner
Harvard Business School

Although all organizations tend to pass through life cycle stages, constructing a framework to describe the growth patterns of churches, at first glance, seems impossible. After all, churches vary widely with respect to their size, location, theology, denominational affiliation, and membership, to name a few factors.

Yet upon closer examination, it is apparent that many churches deal with a number of common issues at similar stages in their development. For example, starting a new church tends to be a very exciting and stressful undertaking for pastoral leaders—regardless of where and when the noble effort is undertaken.

The purpose of this chapter is to provide an overview of the developmental stages of churches and the major issues that usually surface. In so doing, it is hoped that pastoral leaders will be able to understand and anticipate the processes at work in their church and manage their ministries more effectively. As Professor Greiner has stated, "There is still much to learn about processes of development in organizations." This is especially true when it comes to churches.

Overview of Developmental Stages

The church is founded at some point and grows slowly (Start-up). This stage is followed by a period of more rapid growth (Growth) when membership increases significantly. As a result of the church's growth, steps are taken to get organized and delegate responsibilities so that the church's development is not stifled (Consolidation). This is followed by an extended period in which growth tapers off (Maturity). Although the church's growth plateaus, it does not signal a decline in its health.[2] (See figure 13-1.)

KEY FACTORS IN THE DEVELOPMENT OF A CHURCH

Three major factors influence the development of a church: (1) its age, (2) its size, and (3) the roles and philosophy of pastoral leaders.[3] Let's take a closer look at each of these variables.

Age of the Church

The most obvious starting point for understanding the development of a church (or any organization) is its life span. Classifying a church as "young" or "old" or "middle-aged" has a relativistic aspect. A church begun in the early seventies is much older than a church started last week, but it is young compared to one begun in the fifties. The point to remember is that the passage of time affects organizations, just as it does individuals and groups.

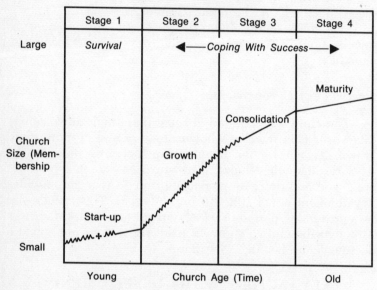

Figure 13-1
Stages of Development

+*Jagged line denotes extraordinarily stressful phases.*

The Size of the Church

The dimension of size is denoted by the vertical axis in figure 13-1. The challenges and opportunities churches face tend to change significantly as a church grows and its staff increases. For example, when Trinity was first established, John (the pastor) had only one part-time employee (secretary) to supervise. Five years later, he had a staff of ten people (full-time and part-time) to oversee. Instead of needing seating for one hundred people, they needed an auditorium for five hundred. In addition, problems of coordination and communication increased.

The Roles and Philosophy of Pastoral Leaders

Autocratic "CEO-type" pastoral leaders thrive during the start-up phase of a new church. After all, they are responsible for everything: teaching, preaching, counseling, finances, publishing the bulletin, and more. The problem with such an entrepreneurial-individualistic style is that it tends to stifle the delegation of significant ministry responsibilities to second-generation pastoral leaders (that is, those who were not part of the founding team) and thwarts team building.

Nevertheless, pastoral leaders who enjoy helping others discover and develop their spiritual gifts will find the latter part of phase 2 (growth) and most of phase 3 (consolidation) a rewarding challenge.

Factors such as a church's theology, the environment in which it is located, general economic conditions, and the proximity of other churches also affect its development.[4]

STAGES OF DEVELOPMENT[5]

Stage 1: Start-up

This is undoubtedly one of the most exciting and challenging stages in the life of a church. As the jagged line in figure 13-1 indicates, church affairs are initially in a constant state of turmoil, which is normal because just about everything is "new" to those involved. The storm does, however, usually subside, and the satisfaction derived from being directly involved in the ministry far outweigh the headaches. The major threat posed to pastoral leaders during this stage is fear of failure, which is fundamentally a challenge of faith. "Will God bless this ministry and cause it to be fruitful?" is a question frequently asked.

Besides faith, pastoral leaders need an extra measure of strength and a will to persevere during this period. Few will

163

forget the special "family feeling" emanating from the fact that everyone is involved. The church's major means of attracting new members during this period is its Sunday morning worship service. In addition, the church has relatively few communication problems during this phase; it is smaller and natural networks suffice.

Coping during the start-up phase of a church is not unlike having a new baby in the house. Though richly rewarding, it is a struggle to survive.

Stage 2: Growth

Churches that successfully negotiate the start-up phase then enter a period of numerical growth indicating that the church has survived and will be dealing with the implications of their "success" for some time to come. One of the first changes pastoral leaders at Trinity made during this stage was to add a second Sunday morning worship service to relieve overcrowding.

Pastoral leaders who are still heavily involved in personal ministry may begin to suffer from "battle fatigue." In order for pastoral leaders to survive this phase and for the church to grow in a healthy manner, it is imperative that church members be equipped to minister. This is especially important because the number and types of ministries begin to multiply rapidly during the later part of this phase. As the jagged line in figure 13-1 indicates, this stage is stretching for everyone. When pastoral leaders rummage through bookstores in search of books on management, it is a sign that the church is entering stage 3.

Stage 3: Consolidation

The rapidity with which a church makes the transition into stage 3 is influenced by the rate and size of the church's growth. If a church triples in size within two to three years (as did Trinity), it will feel pushed to "get organized" sooner than a church growing more slowly. Factors that indicate a church is entering this phase include communication problems, incomplete projects, facilities constraints/building programs, and staff additions.

For pastoral leaders to stay encouraged during this stage and for the church to keep growing, it will be important for them to delegate responsibilities further and to expand the church's small-group ministries. Entrepreneurial-type pastoral leaders who find it hard to give up control (that is, delegate) may find themselves caught in maintaining an institution instead of engaging in personal ministry.[6] Hence, the major threats they face are (1) losing their initial sense of vision and mission for the church, and (2) disengaging after becoming disillusioned with the realities of involvement in a "big" church. This was precisely the point at which several of Trinity's pastoral leaders became discouraged and withdrawn. The seeds of their demise had been sown during stage 2 (growth) when they failed to equip others for ministry.

Stage 4: Maturity

How a church handles stage 3 will largely determine the course of stage 4. Churches that (1) help members discover and use their spiritual gifts, (2) work hard at maintaining communication, (3) use small groups, (4) maintain their sense of mission, and (5) cope with change constructively will find that their body continues to grow in a healthy manner even though its numerical size may level off. On the other hand, congregations that adopt business management methods in stage 3 and neglect the pastoral ministry of the entire body may find that they have lost their "family feeling" and now have an institution sorely lacking in life.

IMPLICATIONS FOR PASTORAL LEADERS

The model described in this chapter describes the growth patterns of many churches. None, however, will go through this particular sequence of stages at precisely the same time or in the same manner. For example, churches

165

with a large proportion of young adults will probably be able to cope with a rapid growth spurt more easily than a relatively "older congregation." The certainty in any case, however, is that churches do change, and pastoral leaders need to be prepared to deal with different sets of problems at different stages. The pivotal factors for each stage are indicated in figure 13-2.

Another certainty is that as a church evolves, pastoral leaders must continually reaffirm their mission. The basic biblical purpose of the church (worship, edification, and evangelism) is timeless. But the "population" which God calls a church to minister to may change significantly—as it did for Trinity.

A third given is that pastoral leaders need to focus their energies on accomplishing what they believe is God's will for them *today*. No one has a crystal ball, and the past is history. It only makes sense to deal with today's "challenges and opportunities" today. Pastoral leaders who abide in Christ have nothing to fear, regardless of what stage they are in (John 15). We need to ask God to help us believe that the future really is as bright as the promises of God.

NOTES

1. Larry E. Greiner, "Evolution and Revolution as Organizations Grow," *Harvard Business Review* (July–August 1972): 37–46.
2. Further information is available in Richard Beckhard and Reuben T. Harris, *Organizational Transitions* (New York: Addison-Wesley, 1987), and Eric Flamholtz and Yvonne Randle, "How to Avoid Choking on Growth," *Management* (May 1987).
3. James A. F. Stoner, *Management* (Englewood Cliffs, N.J.: Prentice-Hall, 1978), 334–39.
4. C. Peter Wagner, *Your Church Can Be a Healthy Church* (Nashville: Abingdon, 1979), explains some of the "diseases" that can affect churches at various stages.
5. Philip Kotler, *Marketing for Non-Profit Organizations*, 2d ed. (Englewood Cliffs, N.J.: Prentice-Hall, 1982), 81–83.
6. Neil C. Churchill and Virginia Lewis, "The Five Stages of Small Business Growth," *Harvard Business Review* (May–June 1983): 30–34.

Figure 13-2: **Key Issues in Stages of Development**

Category	Stage 1 Start-up	Stage 2 Growth	Stage 3 Consolidation	Stage 4 Maturity
Role/style of pastoral leaders	Entrepreneurial "Hands on"	———▲	Delegation and coordination	
Major task(s)	Perseverance	Equipping	Maintaining mission and unity	
Major threat(s)	Fear of failure Lack of faith	Burnout	Disengagement from personal ministry	Loss of vision
Number/types of ministries	Limited	———▲	More extensive	
Facilities	Modest/rented	———▲	More extensive building program	
Church staff	Limited	Larger, more specialized ———▲		———▲
Small groups	Limited	———▲		Increasingly important ———▲
Organizational structure	Simple	———▲	More formal	
Finances	Tight	Good cash flow	Tight	(?)

PART IV

Chapter 14

Pastoral Leadership: Philosophy, Functions, and Blessings

Every church needs a solid philosophical base upon which to build its life and ministry.

Jerry Cook and Stanley Baldwin

Unfortunately, we in the evangelical church are so celebrity conscious that we have a distorted perception of what a leader is.[1]

Richard Halverson, Chaplain
United States Senate

In their superlative book *Love, Discipline and Forgiveness*, Jerry Cook and Stanley Baldwin point out that in the absence of a well-defined concept of how a church ought to operate (that is, a philosophy of ministry), pastoral leaders walk one of three paths: (1) they pastor from crisis to crisis, (2) they adopt current fads, or (3) they subscribe to a concept of church life handed down to them.[2] The problem with such approaches to ministry is that they result in a lot of wasted energy and fail to impart a sense of mission to church members.

In contrast, pastoral leaders who think through how a church should operate (and communicate it to everyone in the church) are able to (1) guide their churches successfully through major transitions, (2) keep more people involved in fruitful ministry, and (3) accomplish their mission.

BASIC ISSUES

It is beyond the scope of this book to set forth an exhaustive list of the issues pastoral leaders deal with in developing a philosophy of ministry. Nor would it be appropriate for me to set forth my views as canon. But all of us, consciously or unconsciously, explicitly or implicitly, have a philosophy of ministry. The underpinnings of this philosophy need to be exposed. Here are three key areas significantly influencing the formulation of a ministry philosophy (fig. 14-1).

Figure 14-1
Developing a Philosophy of Ministry: Key Issues

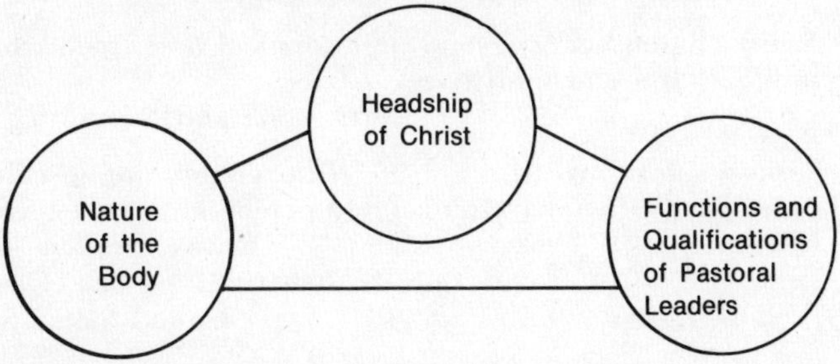

The Headship of Christ

Who is the head of your church? Is it the senior pastor, the pastor's spouse(!), or a key pastoral leader? Have the people been taught to trust God, to put their allegiance in the

172

risen Lord, and to look to him for guidance and direction (Proverbs 3:5–6)? Or do they wander around aimlessly like lapdogs, always quoting "experts," learning of, but never coming to a knowledge of the truth (2 Timothy 3:7)?

One truth the Scriptures make perfectly clear is that Christ is the head of the church, his body. He himself established the church and gave it life (Colossians 1:18). He is "in charge"; he has not abandoned his position of leadership (Ephesians 1:17–23). Larry Richards points out in *A Theology of Church Leadership* that the headship of Christ is evidenced by his love and self-sacrifice for us (Ephesians 5). We need to accept his offering for us and ask him to work in us to replicate his love for the benefit of others.[3] This is the essence of leadership.

Many churches talk about the concept of Christ's headship but ignore it in practice. As a result Christ does not receive the honor and glory he deserves (Revelation 4:11). In addition, many of God's people fail to bear lasting fruit (John 15). Forgive me for belaboring the point, but the greatest single effort pastoral leaders can make is to encourage allegiance to Christ.

The Nature of the Body

How would you describe your church? Is it a warm, friendly place where people are encouraged to grow? Is it a tense, highly structured organization that operates like IBM?

Do the people in your church realize that they are the body of Christ, a living organism that needs all of its members to function effectively? Do they realize that the body cannot function apart from its head (Jesus Christ)? Do they understand that the body grows as its members minister to one another in love (Ephesians 4; 1 Corinthians 12)? Do they realize that the church is a continuing incarnation of the Lord Jesus Christ through which the manifold wisdom of God is being revealed?[4] In short, is being a church member any different than being a member of the Kiwanis Club or the YMCA?

As mentioned earlier, pastoral leaders who do not understand the unique nature of the church seldom train members to use their spiritual gifts and frequently fail to nurture relationships and development of a sense of community. Many adopt business management methods. The church often becomes a vacuum instead of a vibrant community.

FUNCTIONS AND QUALIFICATIONS
OF PASTORAL LEADERS

How does someone become an elder, deacon, or pastoral leader in your church? Are they recognized as a result of their spiritual gifts, ministry service, calling, and character, or are they chosen because of their wealth, social status, and/or education? If it is the latter, how can they lead others to maturity in Christ if they themselves are not mature (Colossians 1:28–29)?

Figure 14-2 (based on 1 Timothy 3; Titus 1; and 1 Peter 5) contains a list of questions to pose to prospective elders or deacons. It highlights the importance of character in Christian ministry. Not all pastoral leaders will be equally strong in every area, nor is anyone required to be "perfect" before they can have a significant pastoral ministry. Nevertheless, Paul felt that the following attributes were important for pastoral leaders: (1) desire, (2) a sound family life, (3) good interpersonal skills and relationships, (4) high moral integrity, (5) a demonstrated willingness to serve others, (6) an ability to teach, and (7) maturity in the faith.

Besides the qualifications listed above, a few practical issues also affect one's ability to function effectively as a pastoral leader. These too should be carefully weighed before one assumes an important position of leadership in the church. First, one must be willing and able to spend time ministering in the church on a regular basis. In other words, the shepherds need to be with the sheep. Not everyone who is *willing* to serve as an elder is *able* to do so because of work or family responsibilities.

Second, highly visible pastoral leaders must be committed to the church, its mission, and its philosophy of ministry. Such commitment is vital to unity, the maintenance of peace, and the development of a sense of community.

Third, a pastoral leader must be willing to be open and honest with others, yet committed to maintaining unity.

Figure 14-2
Qualifications of Pastoral Leaders

1. Does this person *desire* to be an elder or pastoral leader? If so, what is the motivation?
2. Does this person have a sound *family life?*
   a. Does he manage his household well?
   b. Are his children believers?
3. Does this person have good *interpersonal skills and relationships?*
   a. Is he gentle?
   b. Is he quick-tempered?
   c. Is he pugnacious?
4. Does this person have high *morals and integrity?*
   a. Is he holy and devout?
   b. Is he a "one-woman man"?
   c. Is he temperate and sensible?
   d. Is he addicted to wine?
   e. Is he above reproach
   f. Is he respectable?
   g. Is he greedy?
   h. Is he just and upright?
   i. Is he well thought of by unbelievers?
   j. Is he a lover of good?
5. Has this person demonstrated a *willingness to serve others?*
   a. Is he hospitable?
   b. Is he self-willed?
6. Is this person *able to teach* the Word of God and defend the faith?
   a. Is he able to teach?
   b. Is he able to refute objections to basic doctrines?
   c. Is he "holding fast" the Word?
7. Is this person *mature* in the faith (not a new convert)?

References: 1 Timothy 3:1–7; Titus 1:5–9; 1 Peter 5:1–4.

Note: The characteristics listed above are "required" of elders, but may also be used as benchmarks for other pastoral leaders. Love remains the greatest attribute of all (1 Corinthians 13).

Functions of Pastoral Leaders

No two individuals are exactly alike and therefore no two pastoral leaders will have exactly the same ministries. The beauty of the body rests in such diversity; it also underscores the need for participation by all members. There are, however, several major functions in which most pastoral leaders will be involved. Some of these have been dealt with extensively in earlier parts of the book and will therefore be mentioned only briefly here.

Congregational Leadership

More will be said about leadership later in this chapter. For now, it is important to note that pastoral leaders provide congregational leadership by (1) encouraging allegiance to Christ and the purpose of the church, and (2) providing an example (modeling) of Christian living.

Developing a Sense of Community

There is a three-pronged means by which leaders can lovingly and efficiently develop a sense of community. This goal can be achieved by encouraging the development of relationships in the body, establishing small groups, and facilitating communication.

Equipping

The primary responsibility of pastoral leaders is to equip members of the body for ministry (Ephesians 4). This requires an understanding of spiritual gifts and a commitment to the priesthood of all believers (1 Peter 2:19). To paraphrase one author, a pastoral leader's job is not to meet everyone's needs, but to see that everyone's needs are met.[5]

176

Oversight (Administration)

Pastoral leaders are responsible for providing support and encouragement to those who minister. Everyone needs to shoulder a portion of the maintenance functions, but no one is called to drown in details. A major aspect of a pastoral leader's oversight responsibilities involves reviewing ministries, implementing plans, and monitoring progress.

Pastoral Care

The focus of this book has been on management-related responsibilities of pastoral leaders. Therefore, little has been said about familiar aspects of the pastoral ministry such as counseling, comforting those in need, and restoring those who have fallen (church discipline). Nevertheless, these areas remain the heart of the ministry and cannot be overlooked.

Teaching

The New Testament concept of teaching underscores the importance of modeling biblical truths and ministering within the context of loving relationships. Or as Larry Richards says, "Teaching involves bringing Scripture's insights . . . to bear on the lives of body members by instruction, encouragement, advising, urging, exhorting, guiding, exposing, and convincing."[6] The teaching needs of a church cannot be met by a few "experts" (that is, the pastor), nor should one's concept of teaching be limited to formal methods and structures (for example, preaching from the pulpit and classroom instruction). The nature of the church is such that it needs a variety of creative approaches.

Evangelism and Outreach

Pastoral leaders must also train and encourage members of the body to share the gospel and to minister to those in need outside the church. Unfortunately, evangelism often takes a back seat in a number of evangelical churches, and many have shown little concern for social justice and the needs of the poor.

A WORD ON LEADERSHIP

Almost every book on management and the pastoral ministry contains a chapter on leadership. Some focus on leadership *styles*. For example, "democratic" leaders govern by majority rule. "Autocratic" leaders set a course and expect others to follow. "Laissez-faire" leaders are less directorial and tend to accept the status quo.

Some authors emphasize the importance of leadership *traits* such as honesty, integrity, energy, loyalty, and charisma. The theoretical foundation of such discussions is that if one has certain traits, one is qualified to be a leader. There are two pitfalls with such an approach: (1) many people who have leadership traits do not use them, and (2) it tends to create images of elitism as though God, like the marine corps, is looking for a "few good men." Stacy Rinehart, director of the Navigators' Leadership Development Institute, disputes that view:

> God is not looking for just a few good men. He is looking for a multitude of men and women who will bring Him the five loaves and two fishes of their lives, allowing Him to transform them into the broken bread this world desperately needs.[7]

Other books contain extensive discussions on the *origins* of leaders. For example, the essence of the "Great Man" theory is that some individuals are inherently endowed with leadership abilities and are destined to be leaders. George Washington, General Patton, and Winston Churchill are prototypes.[8]

Others ascribe to the "Big Bang" theory, which states that leaders emerge as a result of unique situations and periods of crisis. Abraham Lincoln and Harry S. Truman are frequently mentioned in this context.

The common tension raised by most of these discussions can be traced to a very simple question: Are leaders born or made? The answer is "both." Certain individuals have obviously been blessed with a special measure of leadership gifts, but almost everyone functions as a leader to the extent that they influence others at home, at work, or in the church. And everyone, even bountifully gifted leaders, can enhance leadership abilities by practical experience and training in righteousness (2 Timothy 3:16–17). In short, pastoral leadership is not restricted to a few people, nor does it follow secular patterns. Indeed, the two words that capture the essence of biblical leadership—"shepherd" and "servant"— are seldom found in a secular leader's vocabulary.

Shepherd

Pastoral leaders are first and foremost shepherds. The term *poimen* underscores their devotion to duty (John 10:3–18; Luke 15:4–7). The primary responsibilities of shepherds set forth in the New Testament may be summarized as follows: (1) to care for the spiritual welfare of the flock (Acts 20:28; John 21:15–17; 1 Peter 5:2–4), and (2) to seek the lost (Matthew 18:12–14; Luke 11:23).[9] (See figure 14-3.)

Jesus Christ is the Good Shepherd who was willing to lay down his life for his sheep (John 10:1–30). His special relationship with his sheep (that is, believers) is reflected by the fact that they know him and follow him willingly (Psalm 23). All pastoral leaders should be growing in the likeness of the Good Shepherd (Hebrews 13:20–21).

Figure 14-3
Characteristics of Skillful Shepherds

1. Reject the bureaucratic concept of ministry . . . which has tied the ministry to academic, legal, and prestigious knots from which even Houdini would find it hard to escape.
2. Base their ministry on their spiritual calling, character, and gifts.
3. Are sensitive to the leading of the Holy Spirit.

4. Place their ministry firmly within the body of Christ, and see ministry as a plural exercise on the part of the body, rather than as one man's job (that is, team ministry).

5. See the ministry as a task that demands training.

6. Realize the most essential food on which to nourish the sheep is the Word of God.

7. Will lead the sheep and prepare God's people for ministry so that the body of Christ may be built up.

Source: Adapted from Derek J. Tidball, *Skillful Shepherds: An Introduction to Pastoral Theology* (Grand Rapids: Zondervan, 1986).

Servant

In New Testament times, neither shepherds nor servants (*diakonos*) were highly regarded. In fact, the responsibilities of servants (for example, waiting on tables and caring for households needs) were considered beneath the dignity of freemen (Luke 7:44–47). The Lord Jesus, however, exalted the concept of service. The term *diakoneō* describes "loving action for brother and neighbor, which in turn is derived from divine love . . ." (Mark 10:45).[10]

As an example of the service to be rendered by his disciples, Jesus washed their feet (John 13:15). He also made it clear that leadership among them would not be based on traits, styles, or origins, but on humble service (Luke 22:26; Matthew 23:11).

Paul, of course, expanded the concept of servanthood even further (1 Corinthians 16:15; Romans 12:7). For example, he taught that Christians are servants of the new covenant (2 Corinthians 3:6), of righteousness (2 Corinthians 11:15), of Christ (Colossians 1:7), of the gospel (Ephesians 3:7), and of the church (Colossians 1:25).

In Philippians 1:1 and 1 Timothy 3:8–13, *diakonos* is used to refer to a man or a woman (such as Phoebe, Romans 16:1) holding the office of deacon in the church.[11] The collection of an offering for the saints in Jerusalem (Romans 15:25) and the appointment of persons to meet the needs of widows (Acts 6:1–6) are classic examples of servanthood (Stephen and Philip, for example).

The type of servant leadership embodied in the words "shepherd" and "servant" runs totally counter to the "strong leader" models cherished by society and many churches. (See figure 14-4.)

Figure 14-4
Servant Leadership

	Ruler	*Servant*
Relationships	Over	Among
Command/ attitude	Exercises authority Lords it over	Serves
Major method	Tells	Shows by example
Effect	Behavioral conformity	Heart commitment
Power	Wide range of options	Serves

References: Matthew 20:25–28; 23:8–12; Mark 10:45; John 13:12–17.

THE BLESSINGS OF BEING A PASTORAL LEADER

Shepherding the saints is not easy. In fact, at times it can be downright stressful, inconvenient, and disheartening. Believe me, I have been there. I know what it is like to be misunderstood, to feel unappreciated, to spend hours preparing questions for a bible study only to have the discussion languish, and to care deeply for someone who strays from the fold—and does not return. Yes, at times the ministry can be heartbreaking. But it also has its blessings. Big blessings!

Personal Growth and Maturity

One of the blessings stemming from active involvement in the ministry of the local church is that it acts as a catalyst for one's own spiritual growth. Once you accept responsibility for ministering to others in any capacity you are immediately challenged to live a godly life because of your inherent accountability to God and those you serve. In addition, the

181

process of ministering enables you to develop your spiritual gifts. This brings tremendous results: to borrow a phrase from professional educators, "the teacher always learns more than the students."

Making a Difference

Another blessing associated with leadership is that it enables you to make an impact for Jesus Christ. Of course, no single individual can claim entire responsibility for another person's spiritual growth. To paraphrase Paul, some plant, others water, but in the final analysis, God is the one who causes the growth (1 Corinthians 2:7). But God certainly does use us to help others grow and come to know him.

Unfortunately, many Christians have never experienced the thrill of being involved in what Frank Tillapaugh refers to as "the front lines of ministry." Some have been culturally conditioned to leave the ministry to "experts." Others are too busy with the cares of this life (1 John 2:15–16). Many are afraid they might fail. Hence, they have not experienced the joy of seeing God use them to help others, which is tragic because God blesses our efforts far more than we could ever imagine.

The Satisfaction of Sharing

People obey God for a variety of reasons. Some people obey God because they fear his wrath and the natural consequences of sin (Colossians 3:25). For example, one of the results of opting not to use one's spiritual gifts and/or disengaging from the ministry is that both the individual and the body fail to grow accordingly.

Others obey God because they believe God will reward them for their service; if not in this life, then in the life to come. Frankly, this is probably one of the most neglected areas of theological instruction today, but it makes perfect sense to obey God because of one's desire to be rewarded.

By and large, however, most of the people I know who

are actively involved in the pastoral ministry are motivated out of a heartfelt thanks to God for all that he has done for them. They simply want to share with others the joy and meaning God has brought to their lives. Such sharing is immensely satisfying.

ON BEING FAITHFUL

As I look back and think about the pastoral leaders who have ministered to me the most, one fact stands out: most of them were not "ordained." Nor did they have advanced theological degrees. What they did have, however, only God could give them: spiritual gifts, a heart for and sensitivity to people, and a willingness to let God work through them in building his body. They were servants, faithful shepherds. To know such pastoral leaders and to be ministered to by them, is to see the hand of God at work.[12] To be one is to draw closer to God and his people, and to fulfill one of life's greatest opportunities.

NOTES

1. Richard Halverson, *Discipleship Journal* (September 1987): 25.

2. Jerry Cook and Stanley Baldwin, *Love, Discipline, and Forgiveness* (Ventura, Calif.: Regal, 1976), 99–101.

3. Larry Richards and Clyde Hoeldtke, *A Theology of Church Leadership* (Grand Rapids: Zondervan, 1980), 20.

4. Ibid., 99.

5. Cook and Baldwin, *Love, Discipline, and Forgiveness,* 19.

6. Richards and Hoeldtke, *A Theology of Church Leadership,* 132.

7. Stacy Rinehart, "Spiritual Leadership: Who Can Lead?" *Discipleship Journal* (September 1987): 22–24.

8. Warren Bennis and Burt Nanus, *Leaders* (New York: Harper & Row, 1985), 19.

9. Colin Brown, ed., *Theological Dictionary of the New Testament,* vol. 2 (Grand Rapids: Zondervan, 1978), 564–69.

10. Ibid., 544–51.

11. Walter Bauer, *A Greek-English Lexicon of the New Testament and Other Early Christian Literature*, trans. W. F. Arndt and F. W. Gingrich (Chicago: University of Chicago Press, 1957), 199.
12. Derek J. Tidball, *Skillful Shepherds: An Introduction to Pastoral Theology* (Grand Rapids: Zondervan, 1986), 314–38.

Appendix A

Resources for Pastoral Leaders

This appendix is intended to provide pastoral leaders with practical and thought-provoking resources (books, articles, publications, and organizations), which will enable them to minister more effectively. Resources listed here include selections from a broad spectrum of Christian and non-Christian sources. In addition to providing basic bibliographic data, references have been classified, and most are accompanied by brief annotations. Especially helpful or unique references are marked with an asterisk.

GENERAL

Armerding, Hudson T. *Leadership*. Wheaton, Ill.: Tyndale, 1978. A challenging book with helpful chapters on faith and dealing with success.

Spiritual Leadership, Responsible Management

Arn, Win, and Charles Arn. *The Master's Plan for Making Disciples.* Pasadena, Calif.: Church Growth Press, 1982. A very good book on the basics of discipleship.

Greenleaf, Robert. *The Servant as Religious Leader.* New York: Windy Row Press, 1982. A sequel to his classic book, *Servant Leadership* (New York: Paulist, 1977).

Hellriegel, Don, John W. Slocum, and Richard W. Woodman. *Organizational Behavior.* 4th ed. New York: West, 1986. An excellent textbook on the processes at work in organizations.

Packer, J. I. *Evangelism and the Sovereignty of God.* Downers Grove, Ill.: InterVarsity, 1976. A superlative book on the importance of personal evangelism.

————. *Knowing God.* Downers Grove, Ill.: InterVarsity, 1973. An outstanding discussion of the nature and character of God. Essential reading for pastoral leaders.

Sanders, Oswald J. *Spiritual Leadership.* Chicago: Moody, 1980. The revised edition of an old classic. Focuses on aspects of a pastoral leader's spiritual life.

Schaller, Lyle E. *The Change Agent.* Nashville: Abingdon, 1972. Highly recommended for pastoral leaders who desire to be agents of change in the church.

Snyder, Howard A. *The Problem of Wineskins: Church Structure in a Technological Age.* Downers Grove, Ill.: InterVarsity, 1975.

CONFLICT

Augsburger, David. *Caring Enough to Confront.* Ventura, Calif.: Regal, 1981.

Krebs, Richard L. *Creative Conflict.* Minneapolis: Augsburg, 1982.

Robbins, Paul D., ed. "Conflict: Facing It in Yourself and in Your Church." *Leadership* (Spring 1980): 23–36.

White, John. *The Costly Love of Church Discipline.* Downers Grove, Ill.: InterVarsity, 1985. A helpful introduction to a very difficult aspect of church life.

EQUIPPING AND TRAINING

*Greenway, Roger S., ed., *The Pastor-Evangelist: Preacher, Model, and Mobilizer for Church Growth.* Phillipsburg, NJ: Presbyterian and Reformed, 1987. A collection of essays by veteran

186

pastors who have a passion for evangelism. Filled with practical suggestions on the role of pastoral leaders in equipping the saints to share the gospel.

Jacobsen, Lloyd. "Who Decides What Deacons Do?" *Leadership* (Summer 1983): 67–71. Underscores the importance of modeling servanthood and the process of leadership development.

*Muck, Terry C. "Training Volunteers: A Leadership Survey." *Leadership* (Summer 1982): 40–48. Based on a survey of 172 *Leadership* readers. Contains the six most frequent recommendations of church leaders involved in successful training efforts. Very helpful analysis.

*Senter, Mark. *The Art of Recruiting Volunteers*. Wheaton, Ill.: Victor, 1984. A comprehensive and helpful book on how to engage people meaningfully in the ministry.

FINANCES

Accounting and Financial Reporting Guide for Christian Ministries. Published by IFMA, EFMA, ECFA, and CMMA, 1987. An excellent guide for pastoral leaders and a necessity for every church.

Bergstrom, Richard L. "Stunned by an Inside Job." *Leadership* (Winter 1987): 102–110. A heartbreaking article that underscores the importance of establishing prudent financial controls.

Effective Internal Accounting Control For Non-Profit Organizations: A Guide For Directors and Management. Price-Waterhouse, 1982. An excellent and nontechnical overview of basic areas of financial management for nonprofit organizations.

*"Financial Facts of Pastoral Life." *Leadership* (Winter 1987): 130–37. An excellent interview with several seasoned pastors. Illustrates the complexities of managing church finances and the widely varying role of the senior pastor.

GROUPS

Barker, Steve, et al. *Small Group Leaders' Handbook*. Downers Grove, Ill.: InterVarsity Press, 1982. A practical guide to leading small groups, written by an experienced group of Inter-Varsity Christian Fellowship staff members.

Dibbert, Michael T., and Frank B. Wichern. *Growth Groups: A Key to Christian Fellowship and Spiritual Maturity in the Church*.

Grand Rapids: Zondervan, 1985. Contains a wealth of information on group processes, leadership, stages of development, and how to deal with difficult members.

Griffin, Em. *Getting Together: A Guide for Good Groups*. Downers Grove, Ill.: InterVarsity, 1977. Discusses different styles of leadership, decision making, and member types.

MANAGEMENT AND LEADERSHIP

Anderson, James D., and Ezra E. Jones. *The Management of the Ministry*. New York: Harper & Row, 1978. An excellent book on parish ministry, written by two consultants-clergymen associated with the Alban Institute.

Anderson Paul. "Who's in Charge Here?" *Pastoral Renewal* (June 1985): 161, 172–74. A practical discussion of a body-life approach to leadership and decision making.

Hellriegel, Don., and John W. Slocum, Jr. *Management*. New York: Addison-Wesley, 1986. One of the best management textbooks on the market. Provides an excellent overview of management processes. A great book for those who have never had a course in management.

Hickman, Craig R., and Michael A. Silva. *Creating Excellence*. New York: New American Library, 1985. An outstanding book explaining how leaders can help to develop excellent organizations. Great to read in conjunction with *In Search of Excellence*.

Lindgren, Lavin J., and Norman Shawchuck. *Management for Your Church*. Nashville: Abingdon, 1977. A thought-provoking book that analyzes the church from a systems framework.

Perry, Lloyd, and Norman Shawchuck. *Revitalizing the Twentieth-Century Church*. Chicago: Moody, 1982. A compelling analysis of management and pastoral renewal, of the church's mission and how to accomplish it.

Peters, Thomas J., and Robert H. Waterman, Jr. *In Search of Excellence*. New York: Harper & Row, 1982. Discusses eight attributes of excellent companies. Has proved beneficial to many pastors whom I know.

Schaller, Lyle E. *Activating the Passive Church*. Nashville: Abingdon, 1981. Filled with many practical suggestions for getting the entire church involved in the ministry. Especially helpful for churches resisting or struggling with change.

Schein, Edgar H. *Organizational Culture and Leadership: A Dynamic View*. San Francisco: Jossey-Bass, 1985. Analysis of the roles leaders have in shaping the "culture" of an organization, by a leading expert on management, a professor at MIT.

Tidwell, Charles A. *Church Administration: Effective Leadership for Ministry*. Nashville: Broadman, 1985. A helpful and comprehensive overview of ministry management by a professor at Southwestern Baptist Theological Seminary in Fort Worth.

White, John. *The Costly Love of Church Discipline*. Downers Grove, Ill.: InterVarsity, 1985. A helpful introduction to a very difficult aspect of church life.

* _____. *Excellence in Leadership: Reaching Goals With Prayer, Courage, and Determination*. Downers Grove, Ill.: InterVarsity, 1986. Based on the struggles of Nehemiah, and one of the best books in print.

MARKETING

*Kotler, Philip. *Marketing for Non-Profit Organizations*. 2d ed. Englewood Cliffs, N.J.: Prentice-Hall, 1982. Everything you want to know about marketing and its unique role in nonprofit organizations.

Levitt, Theodore. "Marketing Myopia." *Harvard Business Review* (July–August 1980). Underscores the importance of being continually concerned about customer needs. Primarily geared toward business concerns, but has significant implications for pastoral leaders.

Ries, Al, and Jack Trout. *Positioning: The Battle for Your Mind*. New York: Warner, 1981. A book by two advertising executives that will challenge you to think about how your group or organization is perceived.

PHILOSOPHY OF MINISTRY

*Anderson, Ray S. *Minding God's Business*. Grand Rapids: Eerdmans, 1986. Written as an outgrowth of the Institute For Christian Organizational Management at Fuller Theological Seminary. Explains the importance of management to the mission of Christian organizations.

Getz, Gene A. *Sharpening the Focus of the Church*. Wheaton, Ill.: Victor, 1984. A thorough revision of an earlier work. A challenging perspective on church planting and pastoral renewal.

*Halverson, Richard C. "Planting Seeds and Watching Them Grow." *Leadership* (Fall 1980): 12–23. An interview with the former pastor of Fourth Presbyterian Church in Washington, D.C., and one of the best primers on the pastoral ministry.

"Into the Next Century: Trends Facing the Church." *Christianity Today* (17 January 1986): 1–31. Compiled by fellows and resource scholars of the Christianity Today Institute, an excellent series of essays addressing some of the biggest issues that will "influence the course of the church in the remainder of the twentieth century."

Larsen, Bruce. "None of Us Are Sinners Emeritus." *Leadership* (Fall 1984): 12–23. Underscores the importance of pastoral leaders being vulnerable, and the role of the church as a healing community.

Miller, C. John. *Outgrowing the Ingrown Church.* Grand Rapids: Zondervan, 1986. Shows how one church has fulfilled its mission by creatively adapting to change while remaining faithful to biblical concerns.

*Peterson, Eugene. "Haphazardly Intent: An Approach to Pastoring." *Leadership* (Winter 1981): 12–24. An informative interview with a quintessential pastor. Explains how to balance pastoral-managerial roles.

*Richards, Lawrence, and Clyde Hoeldtke. *A Theology of Church Leadership.* Grand Rapids: Zondervan, 1980. Clarifies the difference between managing a corporation (enterprise) and the church (the body of Christ). An indispensable resource.

*Schuller, Robert H. *Your Church Has Real Possibilities.* Ventura, Calif.: Regal, 1986. A delightfully readable expression of the author's philosophy of ministry. Contains numerous principles and suggestions that can enable pastoral leaders to reach the unchurched more effectively.

*Stedman, Ray C. *Body Life.* Glendale, Calif.: Regal, 1972. Defines and illustrates the biblical pattern for ministry in the local church. A classic!

Stevens, R. Paul. *Liberating the Laity: Equipping All the Saints for Ministry.* Downers Grove, Ill.: InterVarsity, 1985. Illustrates how laypeople are often discouraged from personal ministry by existing church structures and philosophy.

*Tidball, Derek J. *Skillful Shepherds: An Introduction to Pastoral Theology.* Grand Rapids: Zondervan, 1986. Outlines the biblical basis of the pastoral ministry and its development in the history of the church, and discusses five of the most important issues facing the evangelical church today. Essential reading for pastoral leaders.

*Tillapaugh, Frank. *The Church Unleashed.* Ventura, Calif.: Regal, 1982. A challenging and practical discussion of how church members can be mobilized for ministry.

Williamson, Peter S., and Kevin Perrotta, eds. *Summons to Faith and Renewal.* Ann Arbor, Mich.: Servant, 1983. A clarion call to the importance of pastoral renewal and the role of the church in society.

PLANNING

Dayton, Edward R. *God's Purpose/Man's Plans.* Monrovia, Calif.: World Vision/MARC, 1982. A detailed guide to planning based on PERT techniques. Well suited to managers who must develop extensive plans in Christian organizations.

Friesen, Garry, and J. Robin Maxson. *Decision Making and the Will of God.* Portland, Oreg.: Multnomah, 1981. An excellent, biblically based discussion of God's will and its relationship to planning and decision making.

Schaller, Lyle E. *Effective Church Planning.* Nashville: Abingdon, 1979. Sets forth seven basic concepts of planning and leading the church.

*Wagner, C. Peter. *Strategies for Church Growth.* Ventura, Calif.: Regal, 1987. Perhaps the best statement of Peter Wagner's philosophy of ministry as it relates to church growth. Provides a basis for the legitimacy of planning and strategy development.

RELATIONSHIPS

Engel, James. *How Can I Get Them to Listen?* Grand Rapids: Zondervan, 1977. A good handbook on communication.

*Huttenlocker, Keith. *Becoming the Family of God.* Grand Rapids: Zondervan, 1986. Contains a number of creative and practical approaches to developing healthy relationships in the church.

McGinnis, Alan L. *The Friendship Factor.* Minneapolis: Augsburg, 1979. One of the best books available on the basics of establishing and maintaining good relationships. Recommended for every pastoral leader.

White, John. *The Fight*. Downers Grove, Ill.: InterVarsity, 1978. Explains how one's relationship with God changes one's relationship with others.

ORGANIZATIONS

The Alban Institute. 4125 Nebraska Ave., Washington, DC 20016. Phone: (202) 244-7320. Executive director: Rev. Loren Mead. Affiliated with the Episcopal Church. Sponsors numerous educational events throughout the year for pastoral leaders and has an extensive publications program dealing with a variety of ministry issues.

Center for Christian Leadership. Dallas Theological Seminary, 3909 Swiss Ave., Dallas, TX 75204. Phone: (214) 824-3094. Executive director: Bill Lawrence. Conducts research and provides leadership training materials and seminars for Christian leaders in all walks of life.

Center for Pastoral Renewal. P.O. Box 8617, 840 Airport Blvd., Ann Arbor, MI 48107. Phone: (313) 761-8505, President: Peter S. Williamson. Established to foster renewal in leaders' vision of pastoral care and the principles and methods for carrying it out. Serves pastoral leaders in Protestant, Catholic, and Orthodox churches through publications, conferences, and leadership seminars.

Charles E. Fuller Institute of Evangelism and Church Growth. P.O. Box 91990, Pasadena, CA 91109. Phone: 1-800-CFULLER; in California, (818) 449-0425. Director: Carl F. George. Conducts workshops on management, leadership, church planting, and spiritual gifts. Publishes the "Church Growth Resource Guide," a gold mine of information.

Christian Ministries Management Association (CMMA). 1930 S. Brea Canyon Road, No. 170, P.O. Box 4638, Diamond Bar, CA 91765. Phone: (714) 861-8861. Executive Director: Sylvia Flaten. A nonprofit professional association of persons involved in the management of Christian organizations. Sponsors an annual convention and publishes a bimonthly newsletter and a number of other publications.

Evangelical Council for Financial Accountability. P.O. Box 17511, Washington, DC 20041-0511. Phone: (703) 938-6006. President: Arthur C. Borden. An association of evangelical, nonprofit organizations requiring the highest standards of financial accountability and disclosure to donors, government, and other interested persons. Issues a seal of membership to qualifying organizations and provides consulting services and information to members.

The Institute for Christian Organizational Development. Fuller Theological Seminary, 135 North Oakland Ave., Pasadena, CA 91182. Phone: 1-800-235-2222, ext. 5342; in California, Alaska, or Hawaii: (818) 584-5342. Director: Walter C. Wright, Jr. Holds excellent seminars designed to help pastoral leaders and Christian organization executives merge "the spiritual concerns of ministry with the practical principles of management, marketing, and communications."

The Institute for Successful Church Leadership. 12141 Lewis Street, Garden Grove, CA 92640. Contact person: Herman J. Ridder. A ministry of Garden Grove Community Church and Robert H. Schuller that hosts seminars and leadership development programs for church leaders.

National Association of Evangelicals (NAE). P.O. Box 28, Wheaton, IL 60189. Phone: (312) 665-0500. Executive Director: Billy A. Melvin. An association representing more than 46,000 churches in about eighty denominations. Maintains an active public affairs office in Washington, D.C., produces a number of publications, and sponsors several outreach ministries.

PUBLICATIONS

*Christian Leadership Letter. World Vision International, 919 Huntington Drive, Monrovia, CA 91016. Editors: Ted W. Engstrom and Edward R. Dayton. A nonsubscription monthly newsletter supported by readers' donations. An excellent resource on management.

Christianity Today. 465 Gunderson Drive, Carol Stream, IL 60188. Published semimonthly. An invaluable source of information about current events and contemporary issues.

*Leadership, A Practical Journal for Church Leaders. 465 Gunderson Drive, Carol Stream, IL 60188, Phone: (614) 383-3141. Essential reading for pastoral leaders, published quarterly by Christianity Today, Inc.

Pastoral Renewal. P.O. Box 8617, 8400 Airport Blvd., Ann Arbor, MI 48107. Phone: (313) 761-8505. A nonsubscription, monthly journal published by the Center for Pastoral Renewal and supported by readers' donations. Contains a wealth of practical information on the pastoral ministry.

Appendix B

Conducting Church Surveys

Every year corporations spend millions of dollars on employee surveys to keep in touch with their workers and to obtain their input. Many pastoral leaders have also found surveys to be an economical way to solicit feedback from church members regarding their beliefs and satisfaction with current ministries. But Virginia Vagt, director of research and planning for *Christianity Today, Inc.*, recently noted, "To be most effective a survey requires careful planning and analysis."[1] This appendix will explain how to conduct an effective church survey. To blend theory and practice interestingly, the process my own church used is described.

STEP 1: DECIDE WHAT YOU NEED TO FIND OUT

No survey can be exhaustive, so it is important to distinguish what you "need" to know from what you would "like" to know. In our case, we felt we needed information in four areas.

1. *Current Ministries:* We wanted to know how people felt about the church's ministries, and what could be done to improve them. For example, did they want more (or less) teaching on Sunday morning? Did they like (or dislike) using contemporary music? Were they pleased with the couples' class? In addition, we wanted to know what needs were not being met.

2. *Attitudes and Beliefs:* Dallas is often referred to as "the Buckle of the Bible Belt," but it also has one of the highest divorce rates in the United States. Therefore, we wanted to find out if church members knew what the Bible teaches about marriage and divorce. In addition, we wanted to know what their convictions were on other social issues and basic Bible doctrines regarding God, the Bible, salvation, and spiritual gifts.

3. *Demographics:* What was the composition of our body? This included items such as age, sex, marital status, and occupation. We also wanted to know if we were becoming a neighborhood church or a regional congregation.

4. *Special Topics:* How did people hear about the church? Did they know who the elders were or what they did? What kind of religious backgrounds did the people in our congregation have?

STEP 2: DESIGN A QUESTIONNAIRE

This was undoubtedly the most difficult and time-consuming phase in the entire process, and the one in which it helped to have an experienced researcher looking over our shoulder.[2]

In spite of laboring many hours to develop clear and concisely worded questions, several had to be deleted because they were ambiguous or deemed irrelevant. Furthermore, when we "pretested" the questionnaire with elders and other church members (ten people), we discovered that it was too long. Instead of taking 15 to 20 minutes to complete, it took close to thirty. More questions were deleted, the wording of others was sharpened, and some were changed to a five-point Likert scale so that the results could be analyzed more quickly.[3] Examples are shown in figure B-1.

Figure B-1
Sample Questions
A Synopsis of Your Beliefs

The purpose of this section is to gain a greater understanding of your attitudes and beliefs regarding God, mankind, the Bible, and other issues.

Please indicate the level of your agreement or disagreement with the following statements. (Circle one response per item.)

1 = Strongly disagree   4 = Agree
2 = Disagree   5 = Strongly agree
3 = Neither agree nor disagree

						Avg.	Var.
1. Jesus Christ was both fully God and fully man.	1	2	3	4	5	4.8	.445
2. A person can earn his way to heaven by doing good works.	1	2	3	4	5	1.2	.474
3. The only way to get to heaven is by placing one's faith in Jesus Christ.	1	2	3	4	5	4.8	.272
4. I have trusted Christ as my personal Savior and have been "born again."	1	2	3	4	5	4.9	.112
5. The Bible is the Word of God.	1	2	3	4	5	4.9	.113
6. The Bible is free from error in the original manuscripts.	1	2	3	4	5	4.7	.535
7. I know what spiritual gifts are.	1	2	3	4	5	3.6	1.099
8. Christians should abstain from the use of alcoholic beverages.	1	2	3	4	5	2.6	1.179
9. There are situations in which divorce among Christians is justifiable.	1	2	3	4	5	3.5	1.342
10. A person cannot lose his salvation.	1	2	3	4	5	4.2	1.640
11. There are certain situations in which abortion is justifiable.	1	2	3	4	5	2.5	1.960

STEP 3: DISTRIBUTE AND COLLECT QUESTIONNAIRES

Distribution

Questionnaires were distributed via the church's small groups and after worship services. Those who picked up questionnaires after church services were provided stamped return envelopes. All other questionnaires were collected by group leaders and returned to the church office.

To encourage participation a cover letter from the Chairman of the Board was distributed with the questionnaires. It underscored the importance of the survey, requested that participants *not* put their names on the questionnaires (to ensure confidentiality), and expressed the Board's intentions to disclose the results as soon as possible.

Collection

The advantages of distributing questionnaires the way we did were significant. In addition to being quick and inexpensive, it guaranteed a high response rate (63 percent).

Small-group leaders were given guidelines for administering the questionnaire and a large envelope for collecting them. To guarantee confidentiality, group leaders let someone else in the group collect the questionnaires and seal the envelope.

We distributed 408 questionnaires over a two-week period. The cutoff date for returning completed questionnaires was approximately two weeks later. To have extended the return period would have reduced the time available to analyze results and prepare for a congregational meeting.

STEP 4: EDIT RETURNED QUESTIONNAIRES

We assumed that everyone who responded was eligible (that is, that they were members of the church), but we had no way to verify it. Of the 255 questionnaires returned, 12 were rejected because they were incomplete. Thus, we ended up with 243 valid questionnaires, which represented 59 percent of the total distributed (and over half of our congregation). Most researchers are pleased with a response rate of 20 to 30 percent.

Our high response rate reflected three things: (1) the efficient distribution and collection of questionnaires, (2) the interest people had in church matters, and (3) the support church leaders gave the project.

Subsequent to the cutoff date, ten people who did not participate were randomly selected and contacted by telephone to see if there were significant differences between their responses and those who participated. No major differences were detected. When asked why they did not participate in the survey, most indicated they either were too busy or had been out of town. (See figure B-2.)

Figure B-2
Sample Size and Response Rate

Questionnaires distributed via small groups	220
Questionnaires distributed after worship services and during singles class	188
Total distributed	408
Number returned by cutoff date	255 (62.5%)
Number of returns rejected due to editing	12 (4.8%)
Total questionnaires used	243 (59.5%)

STEP 5: ANALYZE RESULTS

When we did our survey, personal computers were still relatively novel. Therefore, we were "forced" to use a mainframe computer. This required transferring survey results to coding sheets which were then keypunched and validated by a service bureau. Roughly 75 percent of the coding was done by two people to minimize coding errors.

Fortunately, with the proliferation of personal computers (PCs), most churches can skip the drudgery of working with data decks and mainframe computers. Any IBM PC or Apple with 256K memory will suffice. I like Lotus 1-2-3 (Release 2) because it is easy to use and has all the statistical functions needed.

Organization of data varied according to the type of question. With open-ended questions, we simply listed the responses on a sheet of paper and looked for natural patterns. For example, one of our open-ended questions was, "Is there anything about our church you would like to change?" We received all sorts of answers, but three patterns emerged: (1) parents wanted more activities for young people, (2) many people complained about parking problems, and (3) many expressed a desire to celebrate Communion more often.

Most demographic information was analyzed by calculating averages. For example, the question dealing with age drew the following responses:

Question: Please indicate your age (check one):

No. of Responses		Pct.	No. of Responses		Pct.
2	less than 20 years	.8%	17	40–49	7.0%
138	20–29	56.8%	3	50–59	1.2%
82	30–39	33.0%	1	60 or over	.4%

The average age of everyone who responded was twenty-five years; 57.6 percent were under thirty years old (56.8% + .8% = 57.6%).

Questions (statements) using a five-point Likert scale were analyzed by calculating the average (mean) and the variance for each. For example, the question dealing with Christ being both fully God and fully man had a average of 4.8 and a variance of .445. An average of 4.8 with minimal variance meant that people strongly agreed with the statement "Jesus Christ was both fully God and fully man."

A statement concerning abortion, which read "In certain situations abortion is justified," had an average of 2.5 and a variance of 1.960. An average of 2.5 indicated that most disagreed with the statement. The variance of 1.960, however, implied that a lot of people felt that in some situations an abortion might be justifiable. In other words, responses to that question varied quite a bit. Moreover, in comparison to the question on the nature of Christ (variance = .445), the responses varied over four times as much! Calculating variances is important because it tells you how "solid" the average is.

STEP 6: DRAWING CONCLUSIONS FROM THE DATA

Figure B-1 summarizes the responses to questions we asked regarding attitudes and beliefs. Most reflect conservative views on major doctrinal issues such as justification by faith and the authority of the Bible, but responses differed greatly on issues like the use of alcohol, divorce, and abortion.

We were surprised to find that over 56 percent thought the theology and practice of the church in which they were raised was "conservative." Over 38 percent had become Christians through a church; 27 percent through the ministry of parachurch organizations. Approximately 10 percent had a Roman Catholic background (see fig. B-3). We also learned that 75 percent of the respondents had attended the church less than two years.

Figure B-3
Religious Backgrounds

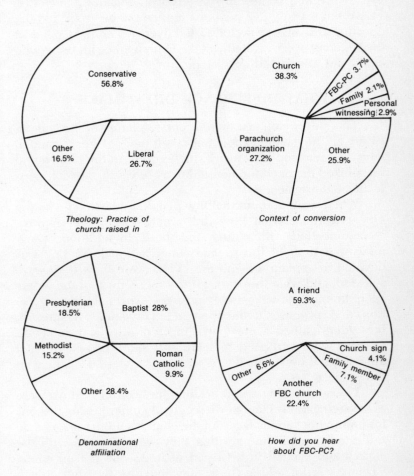

Theology: Practice of
church raised in

Context of conversion

Denominational
affiliation

How did you hear
about FBC-PC?

STEP 7: COMMUNICATE THE RESULTS TO
CHURCH MEMBERS

We felt that the results of the survey were important and
that everyone in the congregation had a right to know what

they were. Therefore we printed a summary of survey results and distributed copies at a special congregational meeting.

About seventy-five people attended the meeting, and the question-and-answer period lasted over two hours! Copies of the summary were available at the church office for those who could not attend the special meeting.

WHAT DIFFERENCE DID IT MAKE?

The elders gained a more accurate picture of the composition of the congregation and their needs. For example, when we realized how many singles were in the church and recognized the need for more ministry to youth, we took steps to meet those needs.

When we found out that few people understood who the elders were or what they did, we took steps to improve communication with church members. In addition, a significant portion of the special congregational meeting was devoted to explaining who the elders were, how they were selected, and what they did. Furthermore, most of the elders spent hours reviewing survey results—especially the suggestions and responses to the open-ended questions. As a result, the elders gained a great deal of credibility and goodwill.

We were surprised to learn that most people did not know what their spiritual gifts were, so we started teaching on the subject.

We gained greater appreciation for how blessed we were as a congregation. Though we received numerous suggestions for improving various facets of the church's ministries, people indicated overwhelmingly that they were pleased with the church and excited to be a part of it. As one person wrote, "Thank you for asking these questions, for desiring growth and maturity in this church. I'm glad to be here."

SUMMING UP

Figure B-4
Overview of the Survey Process

Decide what you need to find out —▶ Design —▶ Distribute and
collect —▶ Edit —▶ Analyze —▶ Draw conclusions —▶
Communicate results

Church surveys are not a substitute for pastoral leaders
maintaining close contact with church members.[4] Nor should
they be done frequently; otherwise church members will tire
of them and resist participating. Nevertheless, surveys large
and small are an effective way to solicit feedback, and most
have members who are willing to help.[5]

NOTES

1. John Vawter, "The Agony and Ecstasy of Feedback,"
Leadership (Summer 1987): 25–27.
2. Further information is available in Gilbert A. Churchill, Jr.,
Marketing Research, Methodological Foundations (Hinsdale, Ill.:
Dryden, 1979), 16–44.
3. Information on developing a Likert scale is available in
Churchill, *Marketing Research, Methodological Foundations*, 102–
124.
4. Philip Kotler, *Marketing For Non-Profit Organizations*, 2d
ed. (Englewood Cliffs, N.J.: Prentice-Hall, 1982), 150–69.
5. To see how a publication uses a survey to solicit feedback
from readers, refer to "Reader Survey," *Leadership* (Summer 1987):
139.

Appendix C

Elements of Productive Meetings

Meetings drive a lot of people crazy! Why? They are frequently poorly led and unproductive. The purpose of this appendix is to provide some practical suggestions for changing that. Every task force/committee is unique, so the following points will need to be adapted accordingly.

START AND END ON TIME

Some people are always late for meetings, and everyone is occasionally delayed by unforeseen circumstances. Nevertheless, meetings should be started on time.[1] To delay is unfair to those who are prompt, usually wastes time, and encourages tardiness.

Furthermore, unless everyone genuinely wants to extend the meeting, adjourn as scheduled. In addition to helping

204

move things along, it eliminates the frustration generated by meetings that drag on beyond their appointed hour.

DEVELOP A USEFUL AGENDA

Distributing agendas prior to meetings provides committee members an opportunity to think through issues before they meet, which helps to expedite the discussion/decision-making process. The problem with most agendas is that they are too brief. Simply listing the topic to be discussed is seldom sufficient, so be sure to include relevant background information.

Including an appropriate heading for each item such as "For information," "For discussion," or "For decision" also provides a sense of direction for committee members.

The agenda should be circulated far enough in advance so that committee members have time to read it. Less organized members may forget about it or lose it, so be sure to have extra copies at every meeting.

The order of items on an agenda is also important. As a general rule, the early part of a meeting tends to be the liveliest, so if an item demands serious attention and mental energy, consider putting it near the top of the list. And by all means, be sure to deal with items that require immediate action first.

CONDUCTING THE MEETING

The primary purpose of the committee chairperson is to facilitate discussions and see that thoughtful, Spirit-led, and practical decisions are made in a timely manner. This requires a great deal of sensitivity to people, an understanding of communication processes, and discernment. At the end of a discussion (or upon making a decision) the chairperson should briefly summarize what has been agreed upon. In addition to helping group members realize that progress has been made, it provides an accurate record for the minutes.

Once an item has been introduced, the chairperson

should (1) encourage a healthy, honest, open discussion, (2) draw out silent members, (3) control the talkative so that they do not dominate the meeting, and (4) synthesize the discussion and clarify the assignment of responsibilities (when required).

One of the biggest mistakes committee chairpersons make is that they fail to terminate discussions early enough. Anthony Jay has stated:

> A discussion should be closed once it has become clear that (a) more facts are required before further progress can be made, (b) discussion has revealed that the meeting needs the views of people not present, (c) members need more time to think about the subject . . . , (d) events are changing and likely to alter or clarify the basis of the decision quite soon, (e) there is not going to be enough time at this meeting to go over the subject properly. . . .[2]

MAINTAINING HELPFUL RECORDS (MINUTES)

A written record (minutes) of every meeting should be made by one of the committee's members and distributed within approximately five working days of the meeting.

Minutes serve three major purposes: (1) they remind committee members of tasks which need to be completed before the next meeting, (2) they help bring those who miss a meeting up-to-date, and (3) they provide a written record of major decisions, etc.[3]

Good minutes are concise, but they should include the following information:

1. The date and time of the meeting
2. A list of all present and absent
3. A list of each item discussed, an accurate description of decisions, and the assignment of responsibilities (who, what, when)
4. The date, time, and place of the next meeting

SUMMING UP

Groups, committees, meetings, etc., are here to stay, and the only way to improve one's skill at leading them is by experience. Try to incorporate some of these suggestions in your next meeting. Time is a valuable gift and doesn't deserve to be wasted in unproductive meetings.

NOTES

1. Mason M. Finks, "Meetings That Work," *Leadership* (Summer 1982): 30–31.

2. Anthony Jay, "How to Run a Meeting," *Harvard Business Review* (March–April 1976): 43–57.

3. James A. G. Stoner, *Management* (Englewood Cliffs, N.J.: Prentice-Hall, 1978), 308–310.